The Fingerprint of God

"God is speaking, are you listening?"

By:

Harold Ball

The Fingerprint of God

"God is speaking, are you listening?"

By:

Harold Ball

Copyright@2015
All Rights Reserved
Printed in The United States of America

Published By:

ABM Publications
A division of Andrew Bills Ministries, Inc.
PO Box 6811, Orange, CA 92863
www.abmpublications.com

ISBN: 978-1-931820-52-3

All scripture quotations, unless otherwise indicated are taken from The King James Version, Public Domain.

DEDICATION

I would like to thank my Pastor Ray Bentley, Pastor Raul Ries, Pastor John Hagee, Pastor Perry Stone, Pastor Mark Biltz, Pastor Dudley Rutherford, Pastor Jonathan Cahn, David Wilkerson, Ray Comfort, Pastor Chuck Missler, and special thanks also to Pastor David Pawson, from whom I've learned so much, *thank you!* And to my friends and family Rick Rivas, Othniel ,Tony Quezada, Golgotha A.R. Churches in Mexico, and Debra Hopkins.

ACKNOWLEDGEMENT

I would also like to extend my gratitude, and give special thanks to my very good friend Mr. A. Maurice Rogers, for his support and contributions to this writing.

HAROLD BALL

TABLE OF CONTENTS

	Special Note From The Author	1
	Introduction	3
1.	God's Signature	5
2	Is The Bible God's Word?	15
3	God's Time Clock	27
4	God's Feast Days	37
5	The Blood Moons	67
6	The Book of Daniel Now Open	81
7	Revelation: *Like You've Never Seen It Before*	105
	Prayer of Forgiveness & Salvation	143
	Final Comments	145
	Ministry Contact Information	147

THE FINGERPRINT OF GOD

A SPECIAL NOTE FROM THE AUTHOR

I am Harold Ball, a servant of Jesus Christ. I came to know the Lord by my brother and Pastor in Christ, Raul Ries of Cavalry Chapel Golden Springs. I am currently under the leadership of Ray Bentley of Calvary Chapel San Diego. I believe we are all predestined by God for service unto Him.

"For we are His workmanship, created in Christ Jesus unto good works, which God has before ordained that we should walk in them" {Ephesians 2:10}. I believe God has chosen me for such a time as this, during this period of the world's history to help get the church ready to meet the Bridegroom.

It all started when I was baptized in the Jordan River in Jerusalem; that was the very beginning of my journey of doing my Heavenly Father's business. I was taught and lead by the Spirit of God, just as Peter and John in Bible days of old. Jesus Christ has equipped me with His anointing, where I received my theological training from H. S. University called by God to be a Watchman.

My accolades are found in the 66 books of the Bible. God has given each of us gifts to be used for His glory, God has gifted me in Bible prophecy and I have spent many years studying it and set myself apart preparing myself to be used by our Lord.

I have learned to discern God's voice as He speaks through His word, and through the many circumstances of my life. I know with God things just don't happen by chance or by coincidences. He has a divine will and plan for each of our lives.

I am not a man pleaser, I live to please God, a man who loves God with all his heart, his entire mind and all his soul.

It is my prayer that the Spirit of God will open your understanding and direct you as you read this greatly needed book....

Harold Ball

INTRODUCTION

In this book I'm going to prove to you that God does exist, and He is living and working today just as He did almost 2000 years ago. He is screaming at the world that He is coming on Rosh Hashanah. Are you ready to meet the King of kings!!!

Let me ask you a question? Do you believe in life after death? (Yes/No). Do you believe in Heaven or Hell? (Yes/No). If you died today, would you go to Heaven or Hell? Why? "Because I'm a good person! I'm not a bad person!" (John 3:3). If you picked Heaven there is a test that you could take right now to see if you are good enough to go to Heaven. Let's take a quiz to see if you are good enough to go to Heaven!

Have you ever heard of the 10 Commandments? (Yes/No). (Exodus 20:1-17). If God were to judge you right now by the 10 Commandments, let's see how you would do. Let's use only four of them! Number 1. Have you ever told a lie before? (Yes/No). What do you call a person who lies? "A liar". Number 2. Have you ever stole anything before? (Yes/No). What do you call someone who steals? "A thief." Number 3. Have you ever looked upon a man or a woman in a lustful way? (Yes/No). God says that "anyone who looks at a woman or man lustfully has already committed adultery within their heart" (Matthew 5:28). Number 4. Have you ever used God's name in vain? (Yes/No). God's last name is not Dammit! You're called a blasphemer!

By your own admission you are a Liar, a Thief, an Adulterer, and a Blasphemer. If God were to judge you right now based on commandment number four or three or two, would you go to Heaven or Hell? Would you be innocent or guilty? "Guilty!!!"

So would you go to Heaven or Hell? You would not be going to Heaven; you would be going to Hell. (Romans 3:10). This is what Christ has done for you! Say you went to court for owing $100,000 in back taxes and the judge asks you to pay it or go to jail. Well you know you don't have a $100,000, so you tell the judge "I cannot pay". So the judge asks the bailiff to handcuff you and escort you to your jail cell. Right before you leave the room a man stands up and offers to pay your fine. The man takes out his checkbook and writes a check for $100,000 dollars and gives it to the judge. The judge says "you are now free." How would you feel about this man that paid the fine?

Would you be grateful, happy, thankful, to this man? That is what Jesus did for you when He died for you on the cross and paid for your sins. He reaches for you, and shakes your hand and says "Will you follow me?" (Yes/No).

Chapter 1

GOD'S SIGNATURE

In this book you will get a glimpse of God as you've never seen Him before.

Most people have never heard or seen God or even witnessed one of His miracles. Today I would like to give you a glimpse into a God that is Omnipotent (all-powerful), Omniscient (all-knowing), and Omnipresent (all-places or everywhere).

Psalms 147:5 says "God is our Lord and mighty in power; His understanding has no limit." God's power is unlimited. He can do whatever He pleases, however, He will never do anything outside of His character. Because God is all-powerful, we can trust Him to help us. We can know that He will always have the ability to do whatever He has promised to do. Without any further ado, let me share with you a little bit of my story and how I got to know Jehovah.

About four and half years ago a good friend of mine, Maurice Rogers, gave me a call and asked me have I been watching the news. He told me that Israel and Iran were about to go to war. I asked him "what day is this?" and then he said this is January 20. I stopped him immediately and said "No! Not our calendar, but on the Jewish calendar?" He said he didn't know. I told him that I would check it out and call him back. One of the biggest reasons I said this was because Jesus was a Jew, and I understood the Jewish calendar. So I went online, and I looked up the Jewish calendar and all I could do is fall back into my chair. Right then and there I knew and asked the Lord, "What do you want me to do?"

Three weeks went by, then one night about 3 o'clock in the morning, then Lord suddenly spoke to me. He said, "Harold, this is the Lord, and I have fingerprints!" While scratching my head, I asked, "What do You mean You have fingerprints?" He said, "I have fingerprints like you have fingerprints." Then I said to Him, "I don't understand what You mean." He said, "My fingerprints are the number Seven." And I said to Him, "I still don't understand." He said, "I will show you what I mean. My fingerprints are all over the world and all over the universe."

He then said, "There are Seven days a week, so who did that?" And I said, "You did Lord." He said, "there are Seven Continents in the world, 1. North America, 2. South America, 3. Europe, 4. Africa, 5. Asia, 6. Australia and 7. Antarctica, and who did that?" I said, "You did Lord." And He said, "There are seven of the tallest mountains in the world, 1. Mt McKinley, 2. Mt Aconcagua, 3. Mt. Vinson, 4. Mt. Everest, 5. Mt. Elbrus, 6. Mt. Kilimanjaro and 7. Mt. Carstensz Pyramid. Who did that?" And I said, "You did it Lord." He said, "I put one of the tallest mountains on each continent 1. Antarctica (Mt Vinson), 2. South America (Mt Aconcagua), 3. Africa (Mt Kilimanjaro), 4. Asia the Tallest (Mt Everest), 5. Europe (Mt Elbrus), 6. North America (Mt McKinley), 7. Australia/Oceania (Mt Carstensz). And He said, "There are seven oceans in the world, 1. Northern Atlantic Ocean, 2. Southern Atlantic Ocean, 3. Northern Pacific Ocean, 4. Southern Pacific Ocean, 5. Indian Ocean, 6. Southern Ocean and 7. Arctic Ocean, and who did that?"

And I said, "You did it Lord."

You see the earth is covered with 70% of water. He said, "You know the best water you can drink is PH7 Pure Water". Even the human body is made of about 70% water. You can't live without water. God says, "Have you seen the rainbow in the sky, the rainbow has seven colors, 1. red, 2. orange, 3. yellow, 4. green, 5. blue, 6. indigo, and 7. Violet. Who did that?" And I said, "You did it Lord." There are Seven (7) Elements of Art 1. Color 2. Value 3. Line 4. Space   5. Shape 6. Form 7. Texture. There are Seven (7) Principles of Design 1. Emphasis, 2. Balance, 3. Unity, 4 .Contrast, 5.   Movement, 6. Pattern and 7. Rhythm. There are Seven (7) Musical Notes A, B, C, D, E, F, and G. Then He said, "There are seven planets in earth's solar system and these are the only ones you can see with the naked eye: 1. Mercury, 2. Venus, 3. Mars, 4. Jupiter, 5. Saturn, 6. Uranus and 7. Neptune. Who did that?" And I said, "You did it Lord."

Then He said, "There are Seven metals in the ground 1. Brass, 2. Aluminum, 3. Cast iron, 4. Bronze, 5. Metal Sludge, 6. Steel and 7. Copper. These raw metals are the most commonly used free from impurities, highly durable resistant to rust, which can endure the highest temperature, 2,000 degrees Fahrenheit, all for you to use, who did that?" Once again, I said, "You did it Lord." And He said, "And I made you in the image of Myself, there are seven holes in your head where you can put your finger in: two eyes, two ears, two nostrils, and one mouth, who did that?" And I said, "You did it Lord". And He said, "Is the only thing you know about blood is that it is the color red? Your blood is made up of seven types of cells: 1. Monocyte, 2. Neutrophil, 3. Eosinophil, 4. Basophil, 5.

Platelets, 6. Macrophage and 7. Erythrocyte, and who did that?" And I said, "You did it Lord." He said, "You thought your skin had one layer of skin but if you look under a microscope your human skin has seven layers and the Epidermis has five Stratum: 1. Corneum, 2. Lucidum, 3. Granulosa, 4. Spinosum, 5. Basel, 6. Dermis and 7. Hypodermis, and who did that?" He said there are seven main parts of the eye: 1. Sclera, 2. Pupil, 3. Lens, 4. Cornea, 5. Optic Nerve, 6. Retina and 7. Iris, "And I did that."

God said that He made speech, and the seven parts of speech are: 1. Nouns, 2. Pronouns, 3. Verbs, 4. Adjectives, 5. Adverbs, 6. Prepositions and 7. Conjunctions, who did that?" God speaks to us in seven ways: 1. Scripture: all Scripture is given by inspiration of God, and is profitable for doctrine, for reproof, for correction, for instruction and in righteousness, that the man of God may be complete, thoroughly equipped for every good work (2 Timothy 3:16-17). 2. The Holy Spirit speaks to our heart: "For this is the covenant that I will make with the house of Israel after those days, says the Lord: I will put my laws into their minds, and I will write them on their hearts. And I will be their God, and they shall be my people. And they shall not teach anyone his fellow citizens, everyone his brothers, saying, 'know the Lord,' for all will know Me from the least to the greatest of them" (Hebrews 8:10-11). 3. The Prophetic: (word of knowledge, word of wisdom, personal prophesy): "Do not quench the Spirit; do not despise prophetic utterances. But examine everything carefully; hold fast to that which is good." (1 Thessalonians 5:19-21). 4. Godly Counsel: "Where no counsel is, the people fail: but in the multitude of counselors there is safety." (Proverbs 11:14). 5. Confirmation: "By the mouth of two or three witnesses every fact may be confirmed" (Matthew 18:16). 6. The Peace of God: "Let the peace of Christ rule in your hearts, to which indeed you were called in one body: and be thankful." (Colossians 3:15), Philippians 4:6-9 "Be careful for nothing; but in everything by prayer and supplication with thanksgiving let your requests be made known unto God. And the peace of God, which passeth all understanding, shall keep your hearts and minds through Jesus Christ. 7. Circumstances/Timing: "After these things he (Paul) left Athens and went to Corinth. And he found a certain Jew named Aquila, a native of Pontus, who had recently come from Italy with his wife Priscilla because Claudius had ordered all Jews to leave Rome. Paul came to them, and being of the same occupation, stayed with them and worked for they were tentmakers by trade. (Acts 18:1-3 – this relationship between Paul, Aquila and Priscilla – which happened as a result of circumstances – became one of the most important strategic partnerships in the book of Acts.

As an interesting side note: God allowed man to create Computer Programming language and do you know how two computers communicate with each other? You would realize the flow clearly when you understand the seven layers of OSI.

The OSI Seven Layers are: 1. Application layer, 2. Presentation layer, 3. Session layer, 4. Transport layer, 5. Network layer, 6. Data link layer and 7. Physical layer. Computer Network is a communication network in which a group or groups of computers and other computing devices are linked together.

God continued to explain many things to me about His

fingerprint being everywhere. God said, "I created all plant life, and there are Seven parts to a plant cell:" 1. Nucleus 2. Cytoplasm 3. Vacuole, 4. Mitochondria, 5. Cell Membrane, 6. Cell Wall and 7. Chloroplasts, and who did that?"

There are seven things needed for them to grow: 1. Room, 2. Water 3. Sunlight, 4. Temperature, 5. Air, 6. Nutrients and 7. Time. Take any one of these things away and your plant will not grow!

God has a great sense of humor, for in the book of Revelation, God lists Seven Churches: 1. Ephesus, 2. Smyrna, 3. Pergamos, 4. Thyatira, 5. Sardis, 6. Philadelphia and 7. Laodicea. Did you know that if you draw a line to connect the Seven churches, starting with Ephesus and then looked down on the world from the heavens, you will see a Seven (7)?

God reigns with man on earth Seven (7) times 1. First, in the Garden of Eden 2. The Tabernacle of Moses 3. The Temple of Solomon, 4. The Temple of Ezra/Herod 5. Jesus the Messiah, 6. The Millennial Temple and 7. The Bride of Messiah (forever).

God created numbers to help us understand that there's nothing impossible for Him to do. When the Lord speaks, He is Mathematically Perfect.

Additionally, here are some more very important numbers you need to understand when you read your Bible: 1 means unity, 2 means union, 3 means Trinity or the Triune God, 4 means creation, 5 means grace, 6 means man, 7 means completion or completeness, 8 means new beginning or a new creation, 9 means fruit of the Spirit, 10 means word of God or the law, 11 means judgment, 12 means government, 13 means Satan or rebellion, 14 means deliverance or salvation, 15 means rest, 16 means love, 17 means victory, 18 means bondage, 19 means faith, 20 means expectancy, 21 means fullness or Father, Son and Holy Ghost, 22 means spiritual knowledge and etc. so what am I trying to say?

Over the next 30 days, the Lord poured into me the signature of God. So I asked Him, "Why are you telling me all of this?" He said, "I want to do two things. First, I want to inform and alert everyone that is not a part of My church, not part of the Bride of Christ, not born-again, to get their house in order before it's too late, for I am soon returning. Second, I want all those that are born-again to know and realize that I know what they are going through, and to hold on, for I am coming." So I said, "Lord they don't know who I am, so they won't believe me." And the Lord said, "Do you remember Moses when I sent him to Pharaoh's house to tell him to let My people go? Didn't Moses say, 'They will not believe me nor hearken to my voice for they will say the Lord has not appeared unto thee?' So I said unto him, 'What is in thine hand?' And he said, 'A rod.' And I said, 'Cast it on the ground.' And he cast it on the ground and it became a serpent; and Moses fled from before it. Then I said unto Moses, 'Take it by the tail.' And he put forth his hand and caught it and it became a rod in his hand again. I did this that they might believe that the Lord God of their fathers, the God of Abraham, the God of Isaac, and the God of Jacob, had appeared to Moses." (Read Exodus 4:1-5).

So, the Lord said to me "Harold, you tell them about The

Seven's and they will know that I sent you." But I said, "Lord, I'm a nobody, why would they listen to me? I don't have a Ph.D. and I never went to seminary school." And the Lord said, "I sent Samuel to Jesse's house where he had seven sons at home, and one was taking care of sheep. All of his seven sons were great men of God and had won many battles."

God continued to say to my heart "Today, I have many great pastors who have led many to Me, but I can't use them. So once again, I have picked a David, and why? The people would give the glory to all the pastors with Ph.D.'s who have gone to great seminary schools. It would be attributed to their education. But when I use a David, the people will recognize that I (GOD) will win the battle. So, I send you, so I (The Lord) can get the Glory. For I will share My Glory with no man." (Ezekiel 33:7 - 'So thou, O son of man, I have sent watchmen unto the house of Israel, therefore thou shall hear the words of My mouth, and warn them for Me.) God has set up watchmen to warn His people throughout history, so listen very carefully and take to heart all the words that I speak to you.

Go now to your countrymen and speak to them. Say to them, 'This is what the Sovereign Yahweh says', whether they listen or fail to listen, give them this warning from Me. God is calling me to warn the wicked, and straighten the righteous. Don't be like the people in the days of Noah, the book of Jeremiah talks about people like that!! Jeremiah 6:16-19 'Thus saith the LORD, stand ye in the ways, and see, and ask for the old paths, where is the good way, and walk therein, and ye shall find rest for your souls.' But they said, 'We will not walk therein (we will not do it).' Jer. 6:17 'Also I set watchmen over you, saying,

Hearken (listen) to the sound of the trumpet.' But they said, 'We will not hearken (don't want to hear).' Jer. 6:18 'Therefore hear, ye nations, and know, O congregation, what is among them. Jer. 6:19 Hear, O EARTH: behold, I will bring evil upon this people, even the fruit of their thoughts, because they have not hearkened (listen) unto my words, nor to my law, but rejected it.'"

In this book I'm going to cover the Seven (7), Fourteen (14), and the Twenty-One (21), God the Father (7), God the Father and Son (77), and God the Father Son and Holy Ghost (777). 777 is found one time in the Bible. I believe that most of the church is sleeping right now, and God wants to wake them up. We worship a God who is living who is operating today in plain sight, so I encourage you to hold onto your seat, gird up your loins, and run towards the finish line.

Let's talk about Jesus (7), who was born in Bethlehem and lived in Nazareth. Before starting His ministry, He walked down to the Jordan River, which is a 77 mile walk, to be baptized by John the Baptist. After being baptized by John, Jesus went up to Jerusalem, which is 777 meters above sea level where later He was crucified. In the beginning, God created the heavens and the earth. In this very first verse of the Bible, (Genesis 1:1) God set the tone for gematria that continues richly throughout both the Hebrew Old Testament and the Greek New Testament.

In Hebrew, this verse has seven words and 28 (7 x 4) letters. The number seven is repeated throughout the Bible as the number of perfection and completeness. 1. In the beginning = 913, 2. Created = 203, 3. God (Elohim) = 86, 4. Eht (aleph/tahv) = 401, 5. The heavens = 385,

6. And = 407, and 7. The earth = 296. Elohim, Heavens, Earth = 777.

Genesis 2: 2, 3 - 2. On the SEVENTH DAY, (7) God ended his work which He had made: and He rested on the SEVENTH DAY (7) from all His work which He had made. 3. And God blessed the SEVENTH DAY (7) and sanctified it..... etc. (777). God the Father (7), God the Son (7), God the Holy Ghost (7). Relative to the six days of creation, 1 + 2 + 3 + 4 + 5 + 6 = 21, Twenty-one equates to a work week.

Chapter 2

IS THE BIBLE GOD'S WORD?

Can we trust the Bible? Is the Bible full of errors and contradictions? Is the Bible just another book?

One of the great questions for today is can we trust the Bible? The Bible tells us that Satan came to kill, steal and destroy. Satan is the father of all lies. We start in Genesis where Satan comes to Eve and misquotes the Bible. (Genesis 2:16-17) "And the Lord God commanded the man saying, of every tree of the garden thou may freely eat: 17 but of the tree of knowledge of good and evil, you shall not eat it: for in the day that you eat thereof you shall surely die. But the woman said, 'God said you shall not eat of it, neither shall ye touch it, lest you die'."

Did the Scriptures say "Neither shall you touch it?." We need to pay attention to Satan's little subtle twist of the Scriptures. Satan has always wanted to destroy God's word from the very beginning of time and even today. Back in history he even tried to get various societies to burn the Bibles, which didn't work. Satan tries to get people to not read the Bible; Then Satan tries to get people to think they can't understand the Bible, so along comes the thought "I'll get you another book to go along with the Bible to help you interpret it, such as the book of Mormon, the New World Translation, or Catechism of the Catholic Church, or maybe The Lamplighter, The Queen James Bible, The New Age Movement, so that didn't work.

Satan even inspired people to write a book for him known as The Satanic Bible. One lie leads to another, and then comes along the new trend to rewrite the Bible. But Satan greatest work ever, is to put hundreds of different translations of the Bible into English. Let me ask you a question? If you came out with a new translation of the Koran what would happen to you in that culture? Or if you came out with a new translation of the Torah what would happen to you? So why do we need so many translations of the Bible other than the King James Version? Why aren't we Christians in an uproar about so many translations!!!! Satan has gotten unaware Christians to buy into a lie, saying that you cannot understand the King James Version, or that Bible is too old and we don't speak like that (in Old English) today, or that Bible has errors and a new Bible will correct those errors.

Whatever lie Satan has told many folks, I'm going to prove today that the King James Bible has no flaws. One example is the NIV Bible Revelation 13:1 "and the Dragon stood on the shore of the Sea." The King James Bible Revelation 13:1 says, "and I (John) stood up on the sands of the sea " My question to you is, *who* stood on the sands of the sea? Was it Satan or was it John? The answer is John. There are numerous mistakes in the NIV Bible translation, but I'm not going to go into all of them at this point. Get Gail Riplinger book New Age Bible Versions to research for yourself.

Some people now say you can't understand the Bible unless you learn Hebrew, Greek, and Aramaic. But I say to those people God made all languages. There are roughly 6,500 spoken languages in the world today however, about 2,000 of those languages have fewer than 1,000 speakers. The language with the biggest population of speakers in the world today is Mandarin Chinese. There are 1,213,000,000 people in the world that speak that language. So if God wanted to speak to me, He knows *my* language. Justice, Genesis, Worship, Creator, Jehovah, Messiah, Blessed, Jubilee, God Head, Trinity, believe, rejoice, Lord God, blessed, baptism, trumpet, forgive, rainbow, promise, forever, Sabbath, TISHREI, seventh, seventy, profit, apostle, shadows, Gentile, servant, brother, witness, forgive, miracle, supreme, wedding, Menorah, mystery, Majesty, eternal, perfect, victory, epistle, rapture, parable, liberty, counsel, SHADDAI, America, Kingdom, awesome, numbers, eclipse, all these have seven letters so do you think he knows my language? He speaks to me in ENGLISH seven (7) letters. If I offered you some Kool-Aid would you want a 100% Kool-Aid or would you want watered down Kool-Aid?

The King James Bible has not one error; it is 100% the word of God. The Bible is not just a book but THE BOOK. it is the living, eternal, infallible, inerrant, indisputable, indestructible, Holy Spirit-Inspired Word of God!!! "All Scripture is inspired by God and profitable for teaching, for reproof, for correction, for training in righteousness: so that the man of God may be adequate, equipped for every good work."- (2 Timothy 3:16-17). "Knowing this first, that no prophecy of the Scriptures is of any private interpretation. For the prophecy came not in old times by the will of man: but the holy men of God spoke as they were moved by the Holy Ghost." - (2 Peter 1:20-21).

Why do I believe that the Bible is the inspired word of God? First of all, the Bible is not just one single book, the Bible is a collection of 66 books that is called the canon of

Scripture. The 66 books contain a variety of genres: history, poetry, prophecy, wisdom, letters, and much more. These 66 books were written by 40 different authors. These authors came from a variety of backgrounds: shepherds, fishermen, doctors, and kings. The 66 books were written over a period of 1,600 years, and many of these authors never knew each other personally. The Bible was written in three (3) different languages Hebrew, Aramaic, and Greek.

Let's just think about this for a moment -- 66 books, written by 40 different authors, over 1,600 years, three (3) different languages, and on three (3) different continents, yet they all carry within them the same storyline: creation, the fall, the rejection of God's people. Also a common theme is God's universal love for all of humanity; and a common message of salvation being available to all who repent of their sins and commit to following the Lord God with all their heart, soul, mind and strength. God's word is truly an amazing collection of writings and letters.

Jason and Ron Carison said after they shared these above facts with a student, they offered him the following challenge: they said to him, "If you do not believe that the Bible is the inspired word of God, if you do not believe that the Bible is of a supernatural origin, then I challenge you to a test. I challenge you to go to any library in the world; you can choose any library you like, and find 66 books that match the characteristics of the 66 books in the Bible. You must choose 66 books written by 40 different authors over 1,600 years, in three different languages, written on three different continents. However, they must share a common storyline, a common theme, and a common message with no historical errors or contradictions." I went on to say, "If you can produce such a collection of books, I will admit that the Bible is not the inspired word of God." The student replied, "But that's impossible."

You see the Bible has been translated into 1,200 different languages, reveals over 250 names of God, and is the world's number one bestseller. When you read the Bible, you read a message from God Himself. When the Bible speaks, God speaks. The King James Bible is the Seventh (7) Bible written in English, 1. Tyndale, 2.Coverdale, 3. Matthew, 4. Great Bible, 5. Bishop Bible, 6.Geneva, 7. King James Version. (Psalms 12:6-7) "The words of the Lord are pure words: as silver tried in a furnace of the earth, purified seven times. Thou shall keep them, O Lord, thou shall preserve them from this generation and forever".

God made everything in six days, and He called it GOOD. At the end of the sixth day, starting the seventh day He called it VERY GOOD. The Bible is written in seven divisions, three are in the Old Testament: 1.The Law, 2.The Prophets, and 3.The Writing; and Four are in the New Testament 1.The Gospels + Acts, 2. Paul's Epistles, 3.The general Epistles, and 4. The Revelation. There are 14 Epistles that Paul wrote and seven general Epistles (21) that are James, 1 & 2 Peter, 1, 2, and 3rd John, Jude, and these Epistles add up to 21 (777) Chapters from these Seven (7) Books.

Back in the early 1930's and 1940's Satan wanted to discredit the Bible. People were saying that the Bible had many mistakes and was changed over the years. But God did an amazing thing, God knew this was going to happen, so God allowed the manuscripts (The Bible) to be kept a cave in Quran, for almost 2000 years for a time like this. In early 1947 (1+9+4+7=21) a Bedouin Shepherd named

Muhammed edh-Dhib (the Wolf) Ahmad el-Hamid and Jum'a Muhammed Khalil, together with their friend Khalil Musa, were searching for a lost sheep, In their search, they crawled through a rock crevice into a cave in the limestone cliffs of the Northwestern shore of the Dead Sea. Instead of a bleating sheep, they heard the sound of breaking pottery. When they investigated, they found Seven (7) nearly intact ancient documents that became known as the Dead Sea Scrolls. Not only did they find seven nearly intact manuscripts they found a whole book of Isaiah in the cave.

You may say what's so amazing about that? The book of Isaiah was translated from Hebrew into English, and it matched perfect word for word to the King James Version. Have you read the book of Isaiah? God preserved it for more than 2,500 years and gave you chapters and verses. God's hand has been on the King James Bible ever since.

The whole Bible has 66 books, and the book of Isaiah has 66 chapters. I call the book of Isaiah the miniature Bible. In the book of Isaiah, the first 39 chapters are "the Old Testament" and the last 27 chapters are "the New Testament." It was as if God was saying "Not only will I give you the whole book of Isaiah, the whole miniature Bible, I am going to number it in chapters for you too."

Let's look at Isaiah chapter 39 as it ends the "Old Testament" and let's start with chapter 40 as it begins the "New Testament" or same the same as Isaiah 40:3, "The voice of him that crieth in the wilderness prepare ye the way of the Lord, make straight in the desert a highway for our God."

Let's look at Matthew 3:3 "For this is he that was spoken

of by the prophet Esaias (Isaiah), saying, 'The voice of one crying in the wilderness, prepare ye the way of the Lord, make His paths straight'." The Book of Isaiah ends with Isaiah 66:22, referencing the new heaven and a new earth and so does the Book of Revelation in the New Testament, (see Revelation 21:1 the new heaven and the new earth). The Book of Isaiah resembles the Bible in miniature, total 66 chapters, 39+27=66, the keyword in the book is salvation. The prophet Isaiah features more Messianic prophecies than any other Old Testament writer -700 years before Christ. Isaiah is quoted in the New Testament for more than any other prophet, being mentioned 21 times by name in the New Testament, WOW!!! God is so Awesome!!!

William Tyndale's translation was the first English Bible to draw directly from the Hebrew and Greek text, the first to take advantage of the printing press, and the first of the new English Bibles of the Reformation. William Tyndale, in the 1530 translation of the first five books of the English Bible, at Exodus 6:3, renders the divine name of God as Jehovah. In his forward to his edition he wrote: "Jehovah is God's name." Tyndale paid with his life so we could have the true word of God.

Jehovah -- does that name ring a bell? Well it should, because that's the name of God also translated as YHVH, the proper name of the God of Israel in the Hebrew Bible. YHVH means behold the hands, behold the nails.

In 1530 William Tyndale printed the first Bible in English with the word Jehovah and the name Jehovah is written in all seven Books. 1) Year 1530 William Tyndale Bible, 2) 1535 Coverdale Bible, 3) 1537 Matthew's Bible, 4) 1541 Great Bible, 5) 1583 Geneva Bible, 6) 1568 Bishops Bible,

7) 1611 King James Bible. Not only is Jehovah in all Seven (7) Bibles, it's in the King James Bible Seven (7) times. All the new translations took out the name of God Jehovah from the Bible. Who told them to take out God's name? Do you think Satan has anything to do with that?

In the Bible in the book of Revelation 22:18-19, God gives a stern warning "For I testify unto every man that heareth the words of the prophecy of this book, if any man shall add unto these things, God shall add unto him the plagues that are written in this book, and if any man shall take away from the words of this book of this prophecy, God shall take away his part out of the book of life and out of the holy city, and from the things which are written in this book.

In 1604, King James of England ordered a new translation of the Bible. With Seven (7) years of labor, 54 scholars, and one of the greatest committee efforts in history, the most widely used book ever written was created. The Authorized Version not only had Seven (7) years of intensely focused effort behind it, but the New Testament had Seven (7) Jewish authors, 1. James, 2. John, 3. Jude, 4. Mark, 5. Matthew, 6. Paul, and 7. Peter.

There are 31,102 versus in the Bible list add them up 3+1+1+0+2=7 WOW!!! The mathematical structure of the Holy Bible has been studied closely in the past, the subject of numerous volumes of writings. However, none are more astonishing than in the works of Dr. Ivan Panin, a Harvard Scholar, Professor, and Mathematician, who once tutored Albert Einstein. His devotion to Christ and years of training as a student in the Scriptures prepared him to be well-equipped him for his future work. For 50 years, Dr. Panin devoted 12 to 18 hours a day to his work. The premise of his revelation is called NUMERICS, proving the divine inspiration of Scripture. They are called Authentication Codes, an automatic security monitor, watching over every single letter of the text, that doesn't rust out or wear out, constantly running through the whole Bible. I called them the Fingerprint and Signature of the Author. Dr. Chuck Missler did a complete study on this same topic, known as Bible Heptadic Structure. Sevens in the Bible occur in over 600 passages, some overt, some structural, and some hidden.

In the genealogy of Jesus Christ found in Matthew 1:1-11, "The number of words must be divisible by seven (7) evenly. The number of letters must also be divisible by seven (7) evenly. The number of vowels and a number of consonants must also be divisible by seven (7). The number of words that occur more than once must be divisible by seven (7). Those which occur in more than one form must be divisible by seven (7). Those which occur in only one form must be divisible by seven (7). The number of nouns shall be divisible by seven (7). Only seven (7) words shall be nouns. The number of names shall be divisible by seven (7). Only seven (7) of the kinds of nouns are permitted. The number of male names shall be divisible by seven (7). The number of generations shall be divisible by seven (7). If you were to work this out it would take you 1,000,000 supercomputers and 4,300,000 years."(This staggers the mind!)

Reftagger says it perfectly "The Bible is unique in its calculation: It is without question the single most published book in the history of the world. It has been read by more people and published in more languages than any other book. Billions have been printed, and tens of millions continue to be so and circulated year after year. Find another book that has stayed on top of the bestseller list for three years or more! The Bible is unique in its translation: It is the single most translated book in the world. Even though it's been translated in over 1,200 languages already; a literal army of full-time translators are working today to make it available to still more people groups. The Bible is unique in its literary durability: It has survived bans and burnings, ridicule and criticism. Countless kings and rulers have tried to eradicate it – but it lives on and its influence continues to spread. Thousands of Bibles continue to pour into Eastern Bloc Countries, the Middle East and Communist China. The Bible has outlived every one of its coolest opponents.

The Bible is unique in its Impact: Over centuries of study, millions upon millions of people have credited the Bible for transforming their lives, altering their view of the world, changing their relationships, altering and impacting their values and their view of eternity. Not many books have that kind of an effect on people's lives. "This Jesus of Nazareth, without money or military arms, conquered more millions than Alexander, Caesar, Mohammed, and Napoleon; without science and learning. He shed more light on things both human and divine than all the philosophers and scholars combined; without the eloquence of schools, He spoke such words of life as never were spoken before or since, and produced effects which lie beyond the reach of orator or poet; without writing a single line, He set more pens in motion, and inspired themes for more sermons, orations, discussions, learned volumes, works of art, and songs of praise and a whole army of great men of ancient and modern times… " - Historian Philip Schaff.

The Bible is unique in its composition: Written over a 1,500-year span, over 40 generations, by over 40 authors from every walk of life, including Kings, peasants, philosophers, fishermen, poets, statesmen, scholars, etc.

The authors include A) Moses, a political leader, trained in the universities of Egypt, B) Peter, a fisherman, C) Amos, a herdsman, D) Joshua, a military general and Moses' predecessor, E) Nehemiah, a king's cupbearer, F) Daniel, a Prime Minister, G) Luke, a respected physician, H) Solomon, a king, I) Matthews, a tax collector, J) Paul, a Rabbi.   It was written in different locations: *Moses in the wilderness * Jeremiah in the dungeon * Daniel on the hillside and in a palace * Paul inside prison walls * Luke while traveling * John on the isle of Patmos * others in the rigors of a military campaign. 5. Written at different times: * David in times of war * Solomon in times of peace. It was also written during different moods: * some writings came from the height of joy and other writings from the depths of sorrow and despair.

It was written on three continents * Asia, Africa and Europe. It was written in three languages: 1. Hebrew, which was the language of the Old Testament. In 2 Kings 18:26-28 it is called the language of Judah. In Isaiah 19:18 it is called "the language of Canaan." 2. It was written in Aramaic, which was the common language of the Near East until the time of Alexander the Great (6th century B.C. – 4th century B.C.) and, 3. In Greek, also known as the New Testament language – which was also was the international language at the time of Christ.

GOD IS SO AMAZING. There are probably 1 to 5 Bibles to be found in on the shelves of many American homes. America loves to buy Bibles, they love to debate the Bible, they love the Bible, they just don't read the Bible!

Chapter 3

GOD'S TIME CLOCK

Is the Bible still relevant for us today?

In fact, the Bible is more relevant today then tomorrow's newspaper. Man writes history after it happens, but God's writes history *before* it happen! Christians refer to this as prophecy. The word prophecy is in the Bible 21 (777) times. Biblical prophecy stands as a stark warning to unbelievers and a blessing to believers that God's fingerprint is all over the Bible. The Bible is 1/3 Prophecy, 1/3 History, 1/3 Salvation. God is speaking, the question is, are we listening?

1 Corinthians 14:3 says "But he that prophesies speaks to man unto edification, to exhortation, and comfort." There are 21 gifts of the Holy Spirit, 7 in Romans and 14 in 1 Corinthians, and 7+14=21 (777). God has given me the gift of prophecy, not that I should boast, but that I give God all the Glory. (A man's gift maketh room for him, and bringeth him before great men - Proverbs 18:16). In Habakkuk 2:1-4 it says, "I will stand up on my watch, and set myself up on the tower, and I will watch to see what He will say unto me, and what I shall answer when I am reproved. And the Lord answered me and said, Write the vision, and make it plain upon the tablets, that he may run that reads it. For the vision is yet for an appointed time, but at the end it shall speak, and not lie; though it tarry, wait for it; because it will surely come, it will not tarry. Behold, is it so which is lifted up is not up right in him: but the just shall live by faith."

When God spoke to me I wrestled with Him, and I said "God if your signature is the number seven, what are you doing today? In the Times Magazine issue of April 8, 1966 on the cover it read in big, bold letters: "Is God Dead?" Then, Dr. Craig's cover story for Christianity Today July 2008 said "God Is Not Dead Yet." I heard a kid once ask why don't we see God doing miracles and signs like He did back in the Bible times? Some of you may you have those same questions. Let's see if God can answer your questions. How many people remember 9/11 and what you were doing at the moment you heard and began watching the news? How many buildings in New York fell that horrible day on 9/11? Well there were seven (7) buildings that collapsed on 9/11. The seventh building that collapsed was not around the other six, it was across the street. There was a big rally in New York regarding the World Trade Center Building, seven (7) people were saying that the "World Trade Building seven didn't just blow Itself Up!." The World Trade Center Building fell down seven hours later in seven seconds (77). The plane that hit the Pentagon was flight 77. The Boeing 757-200 that hit the Pentagon went in at 177 feet.

How tall is the Pentagon? And how many floors does the Pentagon have? The Pentagon is 77 feet tall and has seven (7) floors. God said that He allowed this to happen to America. I asked him why? And He told me that He is sending a warning to America. God always warns his people before He sends judgment. God said, "Because of the homosexuality; because they are taking my Ten Commandments down, because they are taking prayer out of our schools. God said, "I am the one who made America and blessed her and made her a great nation. And now she is turned her back on Me and all My Laws and

Commandments. America has forgotten what I did for her.

Remember the Parable of the Landowner (Matthew 21:33-46) that Jesus told those gathered around Him: "There was a certain landowner (God) who planted a vineyard (Israel), and put a fence around it (protection), dug a winepress in it, and also built a watchtower. Then he leased it to tenants (Jews) and went to another country (heaven). When harvest time had come, he sent his servants (prophets) to the tenants to collect his produce (Christian souls). But the tenants seized his servants (prophets) and beat one, killed another, and stoned another. Again he sent other servants (prophets) more than the first, and they treated them in the same way. Finally he sent his son (Christ) to them, saying, 'They will respect my son' (Christ). But when the tenants saw the son (Christ) they said to themselves 'This is the heir; come, let us kill him and get his inheritance.' So they seized him, threw him out of the vineyard (city walls), and killed him (Christ)." Jesus said "Now when the owner (God) of the vineyard comes, what will he do to those tenants?" They said to Him, "He will put those wretches to a miserable death, and lease the vineyard to other tenants who will give him produce (Christian souls) at the harvest (end of days)." So America is the land that God gave to produce wine (Christian souls). America is that land that God has chosen to be His vineyard.

America has more missionaries, more charities who give the most, more people spreading the Gospel, buying the most bibles, etc. America was founded as a Christian nation. Read about our founding fathers, John Adams, Thomas Jefferson, John Hancock, Benjamin Franklin, Alexander Hamilton, John Jay, Benjamin Rush, etc. all talk about God, Christianity, and Jesus Christ.

President Obama says "WHATEVER WE ONCE WERE, WE'RE NO LONGER JUST A CHRISTIAN NATION; WE ARE ALSO A JEWISH NATION, A MUSLIM NATION, A BUDDHIST NATION, A HINDU NATION, AND A NATION OF NON-BELIEVERS…. The people living in this world deserves to know that this is God's earth. God told Abraham in Genesis 15 that they would be in Egypt for 400 years. God's earth is for good people, and His Holy Land is for holy people. Sooner or later He is not going to allow wicked people to occupy His earth.

The stock market has been crashing every seven (7) years sense 1966. It crashed in 1.) 1973, 2.) 1980, 3.) 1987, 4.) 1994, 5.) 2001, 6.) 2008, 7.) the question is, will it also crash in 2015? These have all occurred on the Shemitah years (Jewish Calendar - The Number 7 Year). 1.)7, 2.) 14, 3.) 21, 4.) 28, 5.) 35, 6.) 42, 7.) 49, and 50 – the Jubilee. The year of Jubilee (Leviticus 25:10) was marked by the fact that all the properties and possessions were given back to the original owner, slaves would be set free; in short, it was a time to "proclaim liberty." A sabbatical year is every seven years. The sabbatical year falls into a cycle of sevens. After every seven sabbatical years, 49 years or 7×7, the first year of a new cycle, or the 50th year, this is a Jubilee year unto the Jews. A Jubilee year happens every 50 years and is called Yovel, which is a time for a new beginning. However, the Jewish nation no longer celebrates the Jubilee year because they do not have all that is required from the house of Israel, the Temple, but, they still observe the sabbatical years.

So, in this manner we can still know when God's Jubilee year for the Jewish nation is to begin. Jubilee means celebration, "At the end of every seven years you can grant a release of debt." – Deuteronomy 15:1. The Hebrew translation of Shemitah is "to release." 3000 years ago when the Lord told Moses, "Six years you shall sow your field, and the sixth year you shall prune your vineyards, and gather its fruit; but the seventh year shall be a Sabbath of solemn rest for the land." (Leviticus 25:3-4).

Have you ever filed a bankruptcy? How long does it stay on your credit? It used to be seven years when you file a Chapter 7. The God of Abraham, Isaac, and Jacob is going to file a Chapter 7 on America and the world. When the stock market crashed in 2001, it crashed on the Seventh month at seven points at 7% (777). Then when the stock market crashed again in 2008, it also crashed on the seventh month at 777 points at 7% (777). The stock market crashed on the seventh (7) month, it was closed for seven (7) days, it was open for seven (7) hours, crashed at seven (7) points at 7%. I count five "sevens." It was on the afternoon of Monday, September 29, 2008, the Congress of the United States was meeting in what was to be one of the most historical sessions in history, not only America but Wall Street, and actually also the rest of the world as well. As the Jewish congressmen were pushing for a roll call so that they could exit and fly back to their hometown and celebrate Rosh Hashanah, the Jewish New Year, the House of Representatives rejected the US $700 billion rescue plan. This was called the "Emergency Economic Stabilization Plan" in order to prevent what was heralded as a widespread financial collapse, in a vote of 228 – 205, a bi-partisan vote including 133 Republicans to 95 Democratic Congressman opposing the bill. That same day the United States stock market plummeted on the average of 777 points; the number of the God of Israel.

Read Jonathan Cahn's book The Harbinger. In it he talks a lot about Isaiah 9: 10-11 "The bricks are fallen down, but we will build with hewn stones: the sycamores are cut down, but we will change them into Cedars. The Lord's reply to your bragging is to bring your enemies against you." On 9/11 the bricks came falling down, when all 7 buildings started falling down just as it says in Isaiah 9.

On July 4, 2004, a 20-ton "hewn" stone was quarried from upper state New York to be installed at Ground Zero with a ceremony, (Isaiah 9 "..but we will build with a "hewn" stones". On September 11, 2001 a sycamore tree was uprooted by debris from the last tower to fall and was later made into a monument called "The Sycamore of Ground Zero." It shielded St. Paul's Chapel at the site Ground Zero where the nation was consecrated to God by the first President George Washington and the first congressional leaders after his inauguration. Not one window was broken in the capital, and it served as a place of rest and refuge for recovery workers at the World Trade Center site. A memorial bronze statue of the uprooted Sycamore was commissioned and installed September 2005 at the end of Wall Street.

May 17, 1792 the New York Stock Exchange was founded by the signing of the Buttonwood Agreement. It was named the Buttonwood Agreement because it was signed under a Buttonwood tree at 68 Wall Street. Buttonwood is another name for the American Sycamore tree. The agreement was from the New York Stock & Exchange Board, now called the New York Stock Exchange. The NYSE became the foundation of the America's, and subsequently the world's economy. (Isaiah 9 "..the Sycamores are cut down."

On November 22, 2003 A Norway Spruce ("Erez" or conifer type tree as is the Cedar) was hoisted by a crane and planted at the very spot of the felled Sycamore at Ground Zero. A ceremony was held, and a new tree was named "Tree of Hope." The 'handwriting' of the prophet was on Wall Street.

Jesus was a Jew, so if you're on the Gregorian calendar you are on the wrong calendar. The Jews use two kinds of calendars 1. Civil Calendar and 2. The Sacred Calendar from which the festivals are computed. The Gregorian calendar has 365 days a year. The Jewish calendar has 360 days a year. The 12 Jewish months are 1. NISAN, 2. IYAR, 3. SIVAN, 4. TAMMUZ, 5. AV, 6. ELUL, 7. TISHREI, 8. CHESHVAN, 9. KISLEV, 10. TEVET, 11. SHEVAT, 12. ADAR/ADARI. Tishrei is the seventh month on the Jewish calendar. On the first day of the seventh month is the feast of Rosh Hashanah. On September 17, 2001 the stock market fell seven (7) points and do you know what day that was? Rosh Hashanah September 17, 2001. On September 29, 2008 the stock market fell 777 points and do you know what day that was? Rosh Hashanah September 29, 2008. Ten days later on October 9, 2008 the stock market tumbled 7%, the Jews celebrated another feast day, and you know what day that was? Yom Kippur October 9, 2008. Five days later on October 15, 2008 the stock market took another tumble seven (7) points, the Jews celebrate another feast day and do you know what that day was? Feast of Tabernacle or Sukkot October 15, 2008 (777). The stock market crashed all on the seventh month of Tishrei all on God's Feast Days.

Thirty days after the stock market crash on October 29, 2008, Cindy Jacobs led prayer for economic recovery around the Golden Bull of Wall Street New York. This reminds me of (Exodus 32) which says "...and when the people saw that Moses delayed to come down out of the mountain, the people gathered themselves together unto Aaron, and said unto him, 'up, make us god's, which shall go before us; for as for this Moses...,' and Moses took the calf which they had made, and burned with fire, and ground it into powder, and scattered it over the surface of the water and forced the Israelites to drink the water".

I am not here to scare you but to warn you that the next stock market crash is coming on Rosh Hashanah 2015. What if you got up out of bed in the morning and you turned on the news and it told you that all the banks are closed, your money is gone, and the money under your pillow that you have stashed is worthless. Not only in America but all over the world, what would you do? What would 7 billion people do? Man writes history after it happens, but God writes history *before* it happens. (Amos3:7) "Surely the Lord God Yahweh will do nothing, but He will reveal to us His secrets unto His servants the prophets".

Most of the world is in recession; the Wall Street Journal wrote an article that asked "Are you prepared for the next crash?" Examiner Steve Forbes says "Link dollar to gold or face Great Depression II." Donald Trump tells Americans to prepare for financial ruin. Pope Francis warns the global economy is near collapse. Jim Richards says "What's your 'day after' plan? 1. Land: every seven years farmers are not to plant crops (Exodus 23:10-11 - Leviticus 25:2-7). This has the ecological and humanitarian purpose 1. Ecological - helps to preserve the fertility of the soil. 2. Humanitarian - for six years you shall plant your lands and gather in its yield, but the seventh year you shall let it rest and lie fallow that the poor of your people may eat. In the seventh year, the poor are free to gather for themselves whatever grows by itself in the fields and vineyards. The year of release 2015.

Let's talk about the storms, and who controls the weather. Who controls the wind, rain, hail, and snow? Does Halle Berry in X-Men, does Zeus, the sky god, does Poseidon the water god, does Mother Nature, maybe El Niño or La Niña, or maybe the secret government Harp. If your answer was any one of these, you are wrong!!! God is in control. Storms, floods, and earthquakes are indeed a part of the present world. We sometimes call them 'natural disasters," but they are no surprise to God. Yes, God certainly can control the weather and send deadly storms. (Exodus 14: 21) "...and the Lord causes the sea to go back by a strong east wind...," (Jeremiah 10: 13) "...He causes the vapors to ascend from the ends of the earth; He makes lightning..." (Job 37:6-7) "... For He the Lord directs the snow, the showers (small rain), and storms to fall upon the earth."

Even the newspapers say that the storms are coming in cycles of seven. Extra! Extra! Read all about it: Forbes magazine October 28, 2012 headline read, 7 YEAR STORM CYCLE: KATRINA, ISAAC, HURRICANE SANDY and THE PERFECT STORM. Even the earthquakes are coming in cycles of seven. Why? Extra! Extra! Read all about it: NEWS HEADLINES: 12/4/2012 Earth booms/ground shaking reported in seven states last 24 hours 1. California, 2.Arizona 3.Texas 4.Oklahoma 5.Alabama 6.Georgia 7.Rhode Island. Extra! Extra! Read all about it: ISRAEL: 10/22/2013 -- Seven earthquakes swarm Israel in 7 Days.

Extra! Extra! Read all about it: JAPAN: 3/23/2011 Tsunami was more than 77 feet high at its peak or about the height of a seven-story building. Extra! Extra! Read all about it: Six COUNTRIES: 4/4/2014 -- Seven Volcanoes In six different countries all started erupting within hours of each other. Almost 7000 miles away in Mexico, the Colima volcano blew its top after a period of relative calm. (LUKE 21:25 "....the sea and the waves roaring") -- Tsunami Killer Wave in 2004 -- Indian Ocean tsunami is considered the most devastating tsunami on record. It is believed then more 250,000 people may have lost lives, many of them washed out to sea. This tsunami was estimated to have released the energy of 23,000 Hiroshima-type atomic bombs, according to the US Geological Survey. The Tsunami's energy traveled as much as 3000 miles to Africa arriving with significant force to kill people and destroy property. Witnesses said the approaching tsunami sounded like three freight trains or the roar of a jet (the sea and the waves roaring). CALIFORNIA DROUGHT: Amos 4:7-8 "...'and also I have withholden the rain from you, when there were yet three months to the harvest: and I caused it to rain upon one city, and caused it not to rain upon another city: one piece was rained upon, and the piece whereupon it rained not withered. So two or three cities wandered unto one city, to drink water, but they were not satisfied: yet have ye not returned unto me, saith the Lord." The Lord declares that storms "do His bidding." Psalm 148:8 God says "Fire, and hail; snow, and vapors; stormy wind fulfilling His Word."

Chapter 4

GOD'S FEAST DAYS

The Seven Feasts of the Lord

In this chapter, we will get a closer look at the Bible in a Hebraic meaning and see through a Hebraic eye. It is good to see the Bible with a Christian eye, but most Christians only have one eye, Their Hebraic eye is closed. Most Jews only have one Jewish eye; the Christian eye is closed. Both Christians and Jews seeing spiritually with only one eye limit their ability to see God's plan clearly. God wants us to see with both eyes and know his plan. The Bible is 1/3 salvation, 1/3 history and 1/3 prophesy. It is good to teach the whole word of God. Most churches teach almost only on salvation, and we rarely get to see the history and prophesy in the Scriptures. Our God is the God of the Jews, and most of us know nothing about our Jewish heritage. This chapter will not only teach you, but it will encourage you and bring you into a more intimate relationship with God. He becomes a more personal part of our lives. Salvation shows us how God redeems us, history teaches us what to do and what not to do. God said, "When you do good I will bless you and when you do bad I will punish you."

Prophesy teaches us to see and shows us God keeps his promises. You get to see his plan in history, salvation and prophesy. The seven feasts of the Lord are 1.the Passover, 2. Feast of unleavened bread, 3. First fruits, 4. Feast of weeks, 5. Feast of Trumpets, 6. Day of Atonement, 7. Feast of Tabernacles. (Exodus 12:14) "And this day shall be unto you for a memorial; and you shall keep it a feast unto the Lord throughout your generations; you shall keep it a feast by an ordinance forever. YHWH SAYS 'THESE ARE MY FEASTS'- (Leviticus 23:2) "Speak unto the children of Israel, and say unto them concerning the feast of the Lord, which ye shall proclaim to be holy convocations, even these are my feasts". (Leviticus 23:4) "These are the feasts of the Lord, even holy convocations, which ye shall proclaim in their season. Passover, Unleavened Bread, Firstfruits and Pentecost are the Spring Feasts and Feast of Trumpets, Day of Atonement and Tabernacle are the Fall Feasts.

The spring feast is the former rain, the first coming of Yeshua and the fall feast will be our latter rain the second coming of Yeshua. The Hebraic name of the Seven Feasts Days are 1. Pesach, 2.Matzah, 3.Bikkurim, 4.Shavu'ot, 5.Teruah, 6.Kippur, 7.Sukkot. The spring festivals: these Feast teach about Yeshua's first arrival: 1. Passover - Jesus is the sacrificial Lamb of God, 2. Unleavened bread - Jesus placed in His tomb, 3. First fruits - Jesus raised from the dead, 4. Pentecost - the Holy Spirit sent. The fall feast teaches about Jesus, Yehshua's Second Arrival: 1. The Feast of Trumpets/Yom Teruah/Rosh Hashanah - The Rapture, 2. The Day of Atonement/Yom Kippur – Armageddon, 3. The Feast of Tabernacles/Sukkot – The 1,000 Year Millennial Reign of Yeshua.

How do we grow in spiritual maturity with God? In Isaiah 28:9-10 it tells us how we are to grow spiritually. Just like a model relationship between a man and a woman grows over time, we grow in our knowledge and understanding of God over time as well while living our Christian life and walking in a deeper knowledge and understanding of God and His ways. The Bible says "Whom shall He teach knowledge? And whom shall He make to understand doctrine? Them that are weaned from the milk, and drawn from the breasts. For precept must be on precept; line upon line, line upon line; here a little, and there a little."

We are on the wrong calendar; we are on Pope Gregory's Gregorian 365 days a year calendar. We should be on the Jewish calendar that is 360 days a year. In the Bible you will not find January, February, March, April, May, June, July, etc. you will not find Monday, Tuesday, Wednesday, Thursday, Friday, Saturday, or Sunday, they are not in your Bible. So where do they come from? Remember Jesus is Jewish, he is not Mexican, Italian, French, African, American, etc. he is Jewish. Therefore, you can find all the Jewish months in the Bible. 1(Nisan *Esther 3:7,, 2). Iyar *1 King 6:1,37, 3). Sivan *Esther 8:9, 4). Tammuz *Ezekiel 8:14, 5). Av *Numbers 33:38, 6). Elul *Nehemiah 6:15, 7). Tishti *1 Kings 8:2, 8). Heshvan *1 Kings 6:38, 9). Kislev *Nehemiah 1:1, 10). Tevet *Esther 2:16, 11). Shevat *Zechariah 1:7, 12). Adar *Esther 2:7.

Let's look at the Jewish months and the Pagan Gregorian Months 1).Nisan = March-April, 2). Lyyar = April-May, 3). Sivan = May-June, 4). Tammuz = June-July, 5). Av = July-August, 6). Elul = August-September, 7). Tishri = September-October, 8). Marcheshvan = October-November, 9). Kislev = November-December, 10). Tevet = December-January, 11). Shebat = January-February, 12). Adar = February-March. In Isaiah 66:23 it says "And it shall come to pass, that from one new moon to another (month to month), and from one Sabbath to another (Saturday to Saturday), shall all flesh come to worship before Me, saith the Most High". (YAHUWAH = 1.Y, 2.A, 3.H, 4.U, 5.W, 6.A, 7.H. THE MENORAH = 1.M, 2.E, 3.N, 4.O, 5.R, 6.A, 7.H.).

So what is the first month on the Jewish calendar? And why is it so important? Why should these feast days matter to us? That's the Old Testament, I'm not Jewish!!! God in the very beginning before He put man on this earth, set up His time clock. Genesis 1:14 "...and God said let there be light in a firmament of the heavens to divide the day from the night and let them be for signs and for seasons and for days and for years." The word Seasons is Moed in Hebrew and it means Appointed Times and Seasons. It occurs 12 times in 12 verses in the KJV. The word Signs is Owth in Hebrew and means Signal or Warning. The word "owth" is found 77 times in the Old Testament. So God was saying "... let them be for warnings and for appointed times...", etc. Appointed Times means Feast Days. (Leviticus 23:2 "Speak unto the children of Israel, and say unto them, concerning the Feast of the Lord, which ye shall proclaim to be Holy Convocations, even these are My feast."

The word convocation in Hebrew is Mikrah and means a dress rehearsal. It is like God is saying His Feast Days are a dress rehearsal (wedding rehearsal) for the real thing to come. Have you ever been at a wedding when you practice before the real ceremony starts. When we read in the Bible, Exodus chapter 12:2 "This month shall be unto you the beginning of months: it shall be the first month of the year to you." This is the month of Nisan on the Jewish calendar. The RAM is a sign of Nisan, the real New Year, which happens before Passover. And the head of the RAM corresponds to Rosh Hashanah, the head of the year. The shofar (Rams Horn) links to these two cosmic dates. Esther 3:7 "In the first month (Nisan), that is the month of Nisan in the 12th year of King Ahasuerus.....", etc. In the Bible in Esther 3:7 it calls this month Nisan. (Exodus 12:3 "Speak ye into all the congregation of Israel, saying, in the 10th day of this month they shall take to them every man a Lamb, according to the house of their fathers and a lamb for an house." This is the month of Nisan, the 10th of Nisan is Nisan 10th.

Now what happened on the 10th of Nisan? This is the day that Jesus rode into Jerusalem on a donkey. This is the day He whipped the moneychangers out of the temple. How do you know this? Because the Jews worship on the Sabbath day and the Sabbath day was Saturday for the Jews. Sunday would have been the first day of the week for the Jew. The Jews would not have been there at their temple on Sunday the first day of the week. They worship on the seventh day of the week. Starting at sundown Friday night to sundown Saturday night. (Exodus 12:6 "And ye shall keep it (Lamb) up until the 14 day of the same month: and the whole assembly of the congregation of Israel shall kill it (Lamb) in the evening."

Jesus died on the 14th of Nisan or Nisan 14th. The priest would prepare the lamb at 9 o'clock in the morning, and they would kill it at 3 o'clock. (Mark 15:25 states "And it was the third hour, and they crucified him..." (Mark 15:34 states "...and at the ninth hour Jesus cried with a loud voice, saying, Eloi, Eloi, lama sabachtani" which means, "My God, My God, why hast thou forsaken Me?" And Jesus gave up the ghost and died.). On the Jewish clock, the third hour means 9 o'clock in the morning and the ninth hour means 3 o'clock. Again when the priest would prepare a lamb for the altar, it would be at nine in the morning, and when the priests would kill the lamb on the altar, it would be 3 p.m.. When the priest would kill the lamb they would shout "TETELESTAI", which means "it is finished." That was the exact same thing that Jesus said just before He gave up His spirit on the cross and then He died (John 19:30). This all happened on the 14th of Nisan. (Leviticus 23:5 "On the 14 day of the first month at evening is the Lord's Passover) this would've been a Wednesday. Yes Jesus died on a Wednesday. Unleavened Bread (Leviticus 23:6 "And on the 15th day of the same month is the feast of unleavened bread unto the Lord: seven days you must eat unleavened bread). This is the day that Jesus was buried on the 15th of Nisan.

During a Passover meal celebration, the Jews will take the middle matzah and break it, wrap half in a white linen napkin, and then hide it to be found by a child at the end of the night. The child who then finds the matzah will get the prize, which symbolizes looking for Christ and finding Him. The Feast of Firstfruits is recorded in Leviticus 23:10-11, "Speak unto the children of Israel, and say unto them, when ye be come into the land which I shall give unto you, ye shall reap the harvest thereof, and ye shall bring a sheaf of the firstfruits of your harvest to the priest. And he shall wave the sheaf before the Lord, be accepted for you: on the morrow after the Sabbath (Saturday) the priest shall wave. Isn't tomorrow after (Sabbath) Saturday, Sunday morning?!!! Right here it is saying Jesus rose early Sunday morning, the morrow after the Sabbath (Saturday). So Jesus rose from the grave on the 18th of Nissan.

The Bible says like Jonah three days and three nights in the belly of the fish so shall the Son of Man be. Let's count backwards: Sunday morning to Saturday morning is 1 Day, Saturday morning to Friday morning is Two Days, Friday morning to Thursday morning is Three Days, so if it's 7 o'clock Thursday morning He couldn't have died Thursday night. So that means He died Wednesday night, was buried sometime early Thursday morning and was in the grave three days and rose early Sunday morning. So where did we get Friday or Good Friday? This is a Roman Catholic term. Let me put it another way! If today is Friday and I told you to meet me back here in three days what day would you show up? I hope you did not say Sunday. I often hear people say that their time and days are different, that is not the case. God from the very beginning of man set the days in the heavens in Genesis 1:4-5. So you don't have to be a rocket scientist to figure out one day, 12 hours a night and 12 hours a day (Light) 24 hours in a day = ONE DAY. And this pattern has been repeated throughout history til today. You don't have to worry about it skipping a night, you go to work at 8 o'clock AM you get off from work at 5:00 PM and you play with the kids till 9 PM and look out the window and it's still the same day you got up. (Leviticus 23:11 "…….and the priest shall wave it), this is a symbol of Jesus coming out of the grave. 1 Corinthians 15:20 explains "But now is Christ risen from the dead and becomes the Firstfruits of them that sleep."

The Feast of Weeks / Pentecost (Leviticus 23:16 "Even unto the morrow after the seventh Sabbath shall you number 50 days)… This is the day that Moses received the law on Mount Sinai. This is the same day that we receive the Holy Spirit in the book of Acts. God put the law in Moses's hands and God put the Holy Spirit in our hearts. This is Sivan 7 on the Jewish calendar. In Jeremiah 31:33 we read "But this shall be the covenant that I will make with the house of Israel; after those days said the Lord, I will put my law in their inward parts, and write in their hearts; and I will be their God, they shall be my people." Then we find in Hebrews 8:10 "For this is the covenant that I will make with the house of Israel in those days, saith the Lord; I will put my laws in their minds, and I will write them in their hearts: and I will be to them their God, and they shall be to Me a people." What does the word "Pentecost" mean? The English word "Pentecost" is a transliteration of the Greek word pentekostos, which means "fifty." It comes from the ancient Christian expression "pentekoste hemera," which means "fiftieth day." But Christians did not invent the phrase "fiftieth day" (50 days), rather, they borrowed it from Greek-speaking Jews who use the phrase to refer to a Jewish holiday. This holiday is known as the Festival of Weeks, or, more simply, Weeks (Shavuot in Hebrew). It is interesting to note that on the same day Moses came down from the mountain 3000 were slain, on the same day the church was established in Acts 3000 were saved (Exodus 32:28 and Acts 2:41). All these four Feast are known as the Spring Feasts, and Jesus fulfilled these feasts on the exact dates that He, (the Great I AM), gave to us in the Old Testament. He died on Nisan 14th, He was buried on Nisan 15th, He rose on Nissan 18th, and He sent His Holy Spirit on Sivan 7. He did fulfill all these that He promised on the exact day.

Now let's look at the Fall Feast and see if He fulfilled all the Fall feasts on the exact day the Scriptures indicate He was going to fulfill them. My God is the same yesterday, today and forever, Amen. Rosh Hashanah / the Feast of Trumpets / Yom Teruah: This is found in Leviticus 23:24 "Speak unto the children of Israel, saying, in the seventh month, on the first day of the month (Tishri 1) shall you have a Sabbath, a memorial of blowing of trumpets, an holy convocation (dress rehearsal)". At the annual religious celebration, the shofar is blown at the Western Wall on the new moon of Tishrei to celebrate Rosh

Hashanah, the Feast of Trumpets (Psalm 81:4) "Blow the shofar at the New Moon."

Pastor Mark Biltz, founder of El Shaddai Ministries, said most Christians know very little about the Jewish foundation of our faith. This is ironic when you think about it, since Jesus was the consummate Jew in that He fulfilled the law perfectly. While we no longer live under the law, Pastor Mark Biltz, believes that a deeper understanding of these festivals of the Lord and the cultural content from which the gospel of Jesus Christ emerged will help Christians better understand the good news and possibly be more prepared to recognize the signs of the Messiah's return. Rosh Hashanah has 12 names 1. Teshuvah (repentance), 2. Rosh Hashanah (Head of the Year, Birthday of the World), 3. Yom Teruah (the day of the Awakening blasts; Feast of Trumpets), 4. Yom HaDin (Day of Judgment), 5. HaMelech (the Coronation of the Messiah), 6. Yom HaZikkaron (the Day of Remembrance or memorial), 7. The time of Jacob's (Ya'akov), trouble (the birth pangs of the Messiah, Chevlai shei Mashiach), 8. The opening of the gates, 9. Kiddushin/Nesu'in (the wedding ceremony), 10. The resurrection of the dead (Rapture, Natzal), 11. The Last Trump (shofar), 12. Yom Hakese (The Hidden Day). Do any one of these names ring a bell? What about this book Nehemiah 8:2 "...and the priest brought the laws before the congregation, both of men and women, and all that could hear with understanding, upon the first day of the seventh month." (Tishri 1). Nehemiah 8:4 "And Ezra the scribe stood upon a pulpit of wood, which they had made for the purpose, and beside him stood Mattithiah, and Shema, Anaiah and Urijah, Hilkiah and Maaseiah on his right hand, and on his left hand, Pedaiah, Mishael, Malchiah, Hashum, and Hasbadana,

Zechariah, and Meshullam. Seven on the right and seven on the left.

Chapter 8 of the book of Nehemiah is a shadow of the rapture of the church and the millennial reign and being with God forever and ever. Rosh Hashanah is a day of blowing of the trumpet. This trumpet is called the Last Trump. In Judaism, there are three trumpets of God, The First Trump, the Last Trump, and the Great Trump. The three trumpets (shofarim) that mark major events in the redemptive plan of God are associated with days in the biblical calendar. The First Trump is associated with and was seen as being blown by God on the Feast of Shavuot (Pentecost) also tied to when God gave the Torah at Mount Sinai (Exodus 19:18-19).

1 Corinthians 15:52 is associated with and the trumpet is blown on Rosh Hashanah. The Apostle Paul, when referring to the resurrection of the dead happening at the last Trump was using a Jewish idiom for the feast of Rosh Hashanah. Genesis 22 is a primary Torah reading on the day of Rosh Hashanah. The ancient rabbis saw the thickets in the verse as representing the sins of the people. Abraham was going to offer his son Isaac on the altar and there was a RAM caught in the thickets. The left horn is called the first trump, and the right horn was called the last Trump. Last Trump is always blown on Rosh Hashanah. That leaves us with the Great Trump and the third significant shofar in the redemptive plan of God. The great Trump is associated with and is blown on Yom Kippur or the Day of Atonement. In Matthews 24:29-31 it says, "…immediately after the tribulation of those days… And then shall appear the signs of the Son of Man in heaven…

And He shall send His angels with a Great Sound of a Trumpet or Great Trump or (Shofar HaGadol)..."

Rosh Hashanah also known as Yom Hakeseh (the hidden day) is a day that "no one knows the day or the hour". No one knows the day or hour? If I can make a dollar every time someone quotes this verse to me, I would be a multimillionaire. This is one of the most often quoted verses in the Scriptures. When Jesus (Yeshua) spoke this, what He said, is what He meant ... What exactly did he mean? There is a first-century Jewish idiom that will shed much light on what Jesus (Yeshua) was saying to His followers 2000 years ago, and to us today. The Hebrew calendar is based on a lunar cycle and consists of 30 day months; with the month officially beginning with the site of the first sliver of the new moon. All Jewish holidays always fall on the full moon of the month except one. Rosh Hashanah (head of the year) is the only holiday that occurs on the first of the month, during the month of Tishri (September/October). Before scientists understood the cycles of the planets and the solar system, the Jews knew that there was a two day window for the siting of a new moon. The new month could not officially begin until two witnesses reported to the high priest that they have seen the sliver of the new moon.

Once the first two sightings were confirmed, the high priest would sound the shofar to declare the start of Rosh Hashanah. But until these two witnesses came forth, the response from the priest would always be "no one knows the day or hour" of when the holiday would begin. Thus the words of Jesus (Yeshua) become significant here with this understanding. (Matthew 24:36) Jesus (Yeshua) was saying that He would come for His bride at Rosh Hashanah

(Feast of the Ingathering or Feast of Trumpets). His disciples would have understood immediately what He meant. But the meaning has been lost over the centuries as the Scriptures have been separated further and further from the Hebrew roots.

Jesus told us to watch, but what are we watching for? Jesus wants us to watch for the signs in the heavens. Rosh Hashanah Yom Kiddushin/Nesu'in (the wedding day), a Jewish wedding the father chooses a woman or the man chooses a woman. The man would ask the woman to marry him and if she said yes he would immediately say "I'm going away to prepare a place for us". Who said that? Jesus. So the Son went to his father's house and told him that he found a bride. The father would say let's prepare the house for you and your bride. In Jewish weddings, invitations are never given out, so of that day no one would know. So when people would hear a rumor about his marriage and when they would see you, they would ask when are you getting married? Your next response will be "I do not know, but my father knows". Who said that? Jesus. So when the house was finished, the father would say "son you can go with your bride" who said that? Jesus. So as you headed for the town to get your bride, she always had to be ready. Cause she knew neither the day nor the hour that the bridegroom would come.

Now in the arrival into the city they would blow a trumpet and say the bridegroom is coming, the bridegroom is coming. So the bridegroom would take his bride and go way for seven days. This symbolizes the tribulation period or a seven-year tribulation period. In a Jewish wedding, the bride's veil is never removed until after the seven days. This symbolizes we come back with Jesus after the tribulation period the whole world will see Jesus and His bride's face.

Most Jews have been celebrating these feast days for some 3000 years and have yet to understand their truest meaning. The Day of Atonement, or Yom Kippur, is another of God's feast days. (Leviticus 23:27 says "Also on the 10th day of the seventh month there shall be a day of atonement: it shall be a holy convocation unto you; and ye shall afflict your souls, and offer an offering made by fire unto the Lord." (Tishri 10th). Yom Kippur has five other names 1). Face-to-face, 2). The day (or the great day), 3). The Fast, 4). The Great Shofar (Shofar HaGadol), 5). Neilah (the closing of the gates) (see Isaiah 27:13 and Matthew 24:31).

Yom Kippur, the Day of Atonement, comes on the 10th day of the Jewish month of Tishri (September/October). It is the last day of the ten days of repentance and is the most solemn day of the Jewish calendar. It is believed that those who have not been good enough to be written into the book of life immediately on Rosh Hashanah are given 10 days to repent, pray for forgiveness, and do good deeds until Yom Kippur, when their fate will be decided. The entire ten days of forgiveness (Yom Kippur) has been fasting and praying. Because this day is the most solemn day in the year, it is known as "THE DAY". Fasting is one of the most important of the mitzvoth (commandments) leading to atonement. The Torah says three times, "And this shall be to you a law for all times: in the seventh month, on the 10th day of the month you shall practice self-denial (Leviticus 16:29, 23:27, Numbers 29:7); in their traditions, the Jewish understanding interprets self-denial as fasting. For this reason, Yom Kippur is known as "THE

FAST DAY". We also see this in the book of Revelation where John wrote about the church in Smyrna. Revelation 2:8 "And unto the angel of the church in Smyrna write these things, saith The First and The Last, which was dead and is alive…. Fear none of those things which thou shall suffer: behold, the devil shall cast some of you in prison, that ye may be tried; and he shall have tribulation 10 days (Rosh Hashanah to Yom Kippur is 10 days): be thou faithful unto death and I will give you a crown of life (tribulation saints)". Revelation 7:13-14 "And one of the elders answer, saying unto me, what are these which are arrayed in white robes? And whence came they? And I said to him, Sir thou knowest. And he said to me, these are they which came out of the great tribulation, and have washed their robes, and made themselves white in the blood of the Lamb."

While we are looking at the Day of Atonement you might be asking about Revelation 6:10-11, "And they cried with a loud voice, saying, how long, O Lord, holy and true, dost Thou not judge and avenge our blood on them that dwell on the earth? And white robes were given unto every one of them, and it was said unto them, that they should rest yet for a little season, until they are fellow servants also and their brethren, that should be killed as they were should be fulfilled." These are the martyrs, and Stephen was the first martyr, and there will be the last martyr right up to the rapture of the church. These are not tribulation saints; they are martyrs and yes there is a difference. Martyrs die before the tribulation period, and the tribulation saints die during the tribulation period. Notice that they are asking God to send His judgment and God's response is wait till all the martyrs come in and then I was in my judgment. The judgment He is going to send is the

Tribulation. Again notice He says 'I cannot send My judgment until all the martyrs come in, and only then will I execute My Judgment. If He had executed His judgment, the martyrs would not be saying this: "How long O Lord, You do not judge and avenge our blood." He would have already done it and they would have no reason to ask for Him to do it.

I touched on some of the points earlier on the wedding day as representing Yom Kippur, but I discovered a few more parallels to this custom. On our wedding day it is customary for the bride to wear white. They are set to start a new life with a clean spiritual slate and get forgiveness for all sins. For the actual marriage ceremony under the chuppah, the groom wears a kittel, a white garment that can also serve as a traditional shroud. The white symbolizes purity and cleansing of sin, and the remainder of this is also meant to inspire proper spiritual thoughts, which is why men wear kittels on Yom Kippur. Is this one reason why brides wear white on their Wedding Day? Probably.

The Feast of Tabernacle or Sukkot: (Leviticus 23:39) is also on the 15th day of the seventh month, "When you have gathered in the fruit of the land, you shall keep the feast unto the Lord seven days: on the first day shall be a Sabbath, and on the eighth day shall be a Sabbath." This is the millennial reign of Christ Who will rule and reign on earth. This is the thousand year (1000) reign of Christ on earth. This is where Satan will be chained for a thousand years (Revelation 20:1-8). A thousand years is found six times in the book of Revelation, chapter 20. The eighth day symbolizes a new beginning; the number eight means new beginning. (Matthew 26:47-54): "Now in the garden of Gethsemane when they came to arrest Jesus, Peter took out his sword and slashed off the ear of the high priest servant. 'Put away your sword', Jesus told him, 'those using swords will die by the sword, don't you realize that I could ask my father to give me more than 12 legions of angels? But how then shall the Scriptures be fulfilled and thus it must be?'" (What we know in the Old Testament is that one Angel killed 144,000 Assyrians). Is all happening to fulfill the words of the prophets as recorded in the Scriptures? In other words, what Jesus was saying was, I have to die on the 14th of Nisan, I have to be buried on the 15th of Nisan, I have to rise from the grave on the 18th of Nisan, I have to send my Holy Spirit on the seventh (7th) of Sivan, I have to rapture the church on the first (1st) of Tishri, My wedding ceremony is on the 10th of Tishri, I have to reign on earth starting on the 15th of Tishri. I have to do all these things on the exact day as I have said in My Word and as I had promised.

Some people say God could change His mind, yes this is true, but not when He has written a decree. The Bible is His decree and He has stamped His name in blood and sealed it with His signature. God is a God that keeps His promises. The spring feast Passover, Unleavened Bread, Firstfruits, the Feast of Weeks or Shavuot have been perfectly fulfilled in the first coming of Yeshua as Mashiach ben Yosef, and the fall festivals Teruah (Trumpets), Yom Kippur, and Sukkot will be fulfilled in His second coming as Mashiach ben David. Since the first advent fulfilled all of the spring mo'edim to the smallest of details, (Mo'edim means God appoint times), we believe that the second advent portends similar fulfillment as revealed in the fall mo'edim. So after the Tribulation Period God will take His Elect 144,000 Jews home for His Wedding – Matthew

24:31. Elect means chosen, and when God looked at all the races of mankind in the world He chose the Jews to be His people. In other words it is not so much that God chose the Jews; it is more accurate that the Jews through Abraham chose God.

Choosing was not part of God's original plan. Initially all of humanity was to serve the role of God's messengers, but after the fall of Adam, humanity lost that privilege, and it was open for grabs. Only Abraham chose to take the call. If others would have, and they were offered the choice, they too would have joined in this special covenant which was sealed upon the giving of the Torah at Mount Sinai. Isaiah 45:4 "For Jacob my servant's sake, and Israel mine elect..." Isaiah 65:9 "I will bring forth a seed out of Jacob... Mine elect shall inherit it."

So let's look at the Feast of SUKKOT or The Feast of Tabernacles, Leviticus 23:39 "Also on the 15th day of the seventh month, when ye have gathered in the fruit of the land, ye shall keep a feast unto the Lord seven days: on the first day shall be a Sabbath, and on the eight-day shall be a Sabbath." This is a time of great rejoicing and typified the final consummation of the entire plan of redemption. The first new year begins in the autumn, for, at creation, time began with fruit-trees laden with fruit already to furnish food for man.

Genesis 1:29 introduces and establishes the Feast of Tabernacles, or Feast of Ingathering, as it is also called. It was held at the year's end, or the resolution of the year. Some very interesting Bible scenes are connected with this feast. Solomon's Temple was dedicated at the feast of Tabernacles (1 Kings 8:2,65). When Israel returned from the Babylonian captivity, this was the first feast celebrated after the walls of Jerusalem were restored, and was a time of great rejoicing (Neh. 7:73; 8:17,18). Perhaps another reason we should study Sukkot in particular is that we very well may be celebrating it in Jerusalem one day. Zechariah 14:16-18 says "and it shall come to pass that everyone who is left of all the nations which came against Jerusalem shall go up from year to year to worship the King, the Lord of hosts, and to keep the Feast of Tabernacles. And it shall be that whichever of the families of the earth do not come up to Jerusalem to worship the King, the Lord of hosts, on them there will be no rain. If the families of each will not come up in enter in, they shall have no rain; they shall receive a plague in which the Lord strikes the nations who do not come up to keep the Feast of Tabernacle. This shall be the punishment of each and the punishment of all the nations that do not come up to keep the feast of Tabernacles." This is the 1,000 year reign of Jesus Christ on the earth. The 1,000 Period is called The Millennium. The whole Bible is 7,000 of church history. II Peter 3:8-10 "But, beloved, be not ignorant of this one thing, that one day is with the Lord as a thousand years and a thousand years as this one day." (Sunday/Yom Rishon = 1000, Monday/Yom Sheni = 1000, Tuesday/Yom Shliski = 1000, Wednesday/Yom Revi'l = 1000, Thursday/Yom Chamishi = 1000, Friday/Yom Shishi = 1000, = 6000 years leaves 1000 years Millennium Reign of Christ. 7000 Years of Church History or His (Christ) Story.) Don't be ignorant of what Christ is saying in II Peter 3:8-10, "The Lord is not slack concerning His promise, as some men count slackness; but is long-suffering towards us, not willing that any should perish, but that all should come into repentance. But the day of the Lord will come as a thief in the night; in which the heavens shall pass away with a great noise, and the elements shall melt with heat, the earth also and the works that are therein shall be burned up." (God is outside of time but man is inside of time, and time is up) 2000 years of conscience age, 2000 years of law age, 2000 years of grace age, that equals to 6000 years Man's age. Then Satan will be chained up for 1000 years only to be let out after the thousand years have finished, and that equals to 7000 years. After those 7000 years are finished, God will create a new heaven and a new earth thus this is the Eighth (8th) Day. Eight means new beginning.

God's Time Clock

Genesis chapter 1 says "...and God said, 'Let there be light in the firmament of the heavens to divide the day from the night: let them be for signs, and for seasons, and for days and years'." I call God 'Mr. Always' because He has always been there throughout eternity: Millions and Billions of years ago.

A long time ago God had an angel by the name of Satan, which rebelled against God and wanted to take God's throne (Isaiah 14:12-14) "And Satan took one-third of the angels in a rebellion with him." (Revelation 12:4). So God kicked Satan out of heaven and out of all His galaxies and put him on earth. Somewhere about that time the earth was full of dinosaurs or we call them prehistoric animals.

This is what I think happened as I use my imagination: Perhaps one day the second person in the Godhead said "I would like a family" and then maybe the first person of the Godhead replied "Where are we going to put your family?" Perhaps the second person of the Godhead answered "Let's put them on earth". The first person of the Godhead may have said "Let's clean earth up and then We'll put them there on earth".

The historic flood recorded in Scriptures is also recorded by every major culture of the world. So God flooded the earth and killed all the dinosaurs. This explains why the scientists believe that the earth was created millions and millions of years ago and why you can find so many dinosaur bones all over the earth. We read in Genesis 1:2 "...and the earth was without form, and void and darkness was upon the face of the deep. And the Spirit of God moved upon the face of the waters." Looks like the earth was covered with water. Genesis 1:9 "... And let the dry land appear."

If you are wondering if I'm trying to say that there are two floods, yes I am saying there were two floods. I believe there was an initial one when God destroyed all the dinosaurs and then also when God put Noah and his family on a boat and destroyed all mankind. Approximately 700 species of dinosaurs have been named that are different from one another. So out of all the species there would have been millions and millions of dinosaurs. We have the evidence that they are real, so where are they today? Do you think Noah put 700 species of dinosaurs on the ark? No we read in (Genesis 1:27-28 "…. God created he him, male and female created he them. And God blessed them and God said unto them be fruitful and multiply and replenish the earth…." what does replenish means? To put something back, to restock. God uses that same word two times in the Bible (Genesis 9:1 and God blessed Noah and his sons and said to them be fruitful and multiply and replenish the earth. If your Bible does not say this, then get one that does.)

Why did God tell Noah to put the animals on the Ark? Genesis 7:3 "To keep seed alive upon the face of all the earth". God wanted all the animals back on the earth after the flood. So did God say He wanted to keep the seed of all the animals alive? Where are the dinosaurs? Have you ever looked at the dinosaurs and wondered why they were found embedded in rocks and mud under the earth? Have you ever wondered why elephants, giraffes, tigers, have not been found embedded in rocks and mud underneath the earth? Have you ever wondered why the writers of God's word would use the word replenish only two times in the whole Bible. They could have used the word "fill" because they used the word "fill" in other parts of the Bible. But they chose the word *replenish*. Do you think God was telling us something? Remember the King James Version has not one mistake, and God calls it very good. (Genesis 6:3 and the Lord said, my spirit shall not always strive with man, for that he also is flesh: yet his days shall be 120 years). What did God mean by this statement? Well He wasn't talking about age because Methuselah lived to be 969 years of age. He was talking about Jubilee years.

A Jubilee year is every 50 years (Leviticus 25:10-11). Jubilee is found in the Bible 21 (777) times all in the book of Leviticus. So if you multiply 120 X 50 = 6000. God was saying "My spirit shall not always strive with man, for that he is also flesh: yet his days shall be 6000 years on earth. When I look at the Jewish calendar, I see 5992. So what am I saying? From Adam to Abraham or Genesis 1 to Genesis 12 is 2000 years, and from Abraham to the first coming of Christ or Genesis 12 to Matthew 1 is another 2,000 years, that's 4,000 years. From Christ first coming to his second coming is another 2,000 years. When I add that up it as up to 6,000 years. The Bible is a total of 7,000 years of church history. 6,000 +1,000 year millennial reign adds up to 7,000 years. Moses lived 120 years, and he saw the Promised Land from the mountaintop (Deuteronomy 34:1-12).

I believe that the seven day period shows us the 7,000 year period of the Earth's existence. It is also very interesting how prophecy unfolds if we use that time period and consider the following Scriptures among others. 2 Peter 3:8 "But beloved be not ignorant of this one thing, that one day is with the Lord as 1,000 years and 1,000 years as one day". (Perhaps the clue reads: Sunday 1000, Monday 1000, Tuesday 1000, Wednesday 1000, Thursday 1000, Friday 1000 = 6,000. 6,000 + 1,000 = 7,000. Note Hosea 6:1-2 "And let us return to the Lord for He has torn and He will heal us; He has smitten (beaten) and He will bind us up. After two days (Grace) will He receive us in the third day (1,000-year millennial) He will rise us up, and we shall live in His sight."

You see from Adam to Abraham was the Conscience Age, from Abraham to Christ was the Law Age, and from the first coming of Christ to the second coming of Christ is the Grace Age. We are just about to close the Grace age. Sunday/Monday two days, Tuesday/ Wednesday two days, Thursday/Friday two days, Saturday one day. After two days He will receive us, Thursday/Friday two days, 2,000 years + the third day, Saturday one day, 1,000 years we shall live with Him forever. If you have some time, take a look at Wikipedia Year 6000. Let's look at some facts: first, that the Jewish calendar says 5774. The second fact: from Adam to the first coming of Christ is 4000 years. 2000 years X 360 days a year = 720,000 days. 1774 years – 2000 years = 226 years. 1774 years X 360 days = 638,640 days (fact). 7 years X 360 days = 2520 days (fact). 226 years – 7 years = 219 years (fact). 720,000 days = 2000 years (fact). 2,160,000 days = 6000 years (fact). God's calendar is 360 days a year (fact), and the pagan calendar is 365 days a year (fact).

So let's take the Jewish Calendar: if we subtract 4000 years from the year 5774 that equals 1774 (fact). Some Jewish scholars say they have miscounted 219 years. Their calendar is off by 219 years. 1774 years (fact) X 360 (days of Jewish years) = 638,640 Days. 219 (Jewish Years miscounted) X 360 (days of Jewish years) = 78,840 Days. 638,640 Days + 78,840 Days = 717,480 Days. 717,480 Days divide by 360 Days = 1993 (The Year). 4000 years conscience/law age + 1993 years Grace Age = 5993 years. The Jewish calendar should be the year 5993 and our calendar year should be the year 1993 but since our calendar added 5 more days a year to 365 days a year it puts us at 2015 (Pictures). (720,000 days – 638,640 days = 81,360 days). (81,360 days – 2,520 days = 78,840 days). (219 years X 360 days = 78,840 days).

What is the Year of Jubilee? Historically, at the Jubilee, all of the debts were canceled, all of the slaves were set free, and all of the land was returned to its rightful owner. This is a physical example of the spiritual truths that are fulfilled in Jesus Christ, and will be finished at His second coming. The debt of sin is canceled, the slaves of sin are set free, and the rulership of the earth will return to Jesus Christ and His Bride forever. <u>Jubilee is God's Divine Reset</u>.

Let the celebrations begin; some Jubilee years are 1868, 1917, 1966, 2015.

The Balfour Declaration – (Lord Balfour was the British Foreign Secretary) his majesty's government view with the establishment in Palestine of a national home for the Jewish people happened in October 31, 1917. The Mandate for Palestine (British Mandate), April 24, 1920 owned all of Israel with 120,466 Sq. Km. In July 24, 1922 the reconstitution of the Jewish National Home was to be postponed or withheld. The territory of Jewish Palestine has been reduced by 77% of the original mandate; Jewish Palestine got 28,166 Sq. Km 23% which leaves Trans-Jordon Arab Palestine 92,300 Sq. Km 77%. This Declaration was prompted by the fact that during World War 1 the Turks sided with the Germans. And when Germany lost the war, so did the Turks, and the victorious Allies decided to divide up both the German and Turkish empires. The Turkish territories, called the Ottoman Empire, contained the ancient homeland of the Jewish people, an area the Romans had named Palestine after the last Jewish revolt in 132-135 AD. By dividing up the German and Turkish territories, Britain was allotted Palestine, and this is what prompted the Balfour Declaration. In that document, Lord Balfour, the British Foreign Secretary, declared that it was the intention of the British government to establish in Palestine "a national home for the Jewish people."

In 1922 the League of Nations gave Britain the Mandate to see this national homeland implemented. But almost Immediately Britain cut away 77% of the original mandated area for the Jews to create what later became known as Jordan. During the year of 1917 there were a total of Seven (7) Eclipses (4 eclipses of the sun; 3 of the moon): (1.) Jan 08, (2.) Jan 23, (3.) Jun 19, (4.) Jul 04, (5.) Jul 19, (6.) Dec. 14, (7.) Dec. 28. Seven is the most eclipses you can have in a one year period.

Isaiah prophesied that Israel would become a nation again and that it would happen in one day! Isaiah wrote about this perhaps between 701-681 BC and it was fulfilled in 1948. (Isaiah 66:7-8 "Before she travailed, she brought forth, before her pain came, she was delivered of a man child. Who has heard such a thing? Who has seen such a thing? Or shall a nation be born at once? For as soon as Zion travailed, she brought forth her children." In 1948 Israel got the land back and there were four blood moons and we call them Tetrad. But before we talk about the blood moons let's see what Jesus said about His second coming. Matthew 24:1 "...and Jesus went out, and departed from the Temple: and His disciples came to Him for to show Him the building of the temple." You see here in this passage the disciples were showing Jesus the Temple and how beautiful it was. Matthew 24:2 "...and Jesus said to them, 'Do you not see all these things? Verily I say unto you there should not be left here one stone upon another that shall not be thrown down'." Jesus was prophesying about things to come. In Titus the Roman Emperor destroyed Jerusalem in 70 A.D. Matthew 24:3 "...and as He sat on the Mount of Olives, the disciples came to Him privately, saying, tell us, when shall these things be? And what shall be the sign of Thy coming, and of the end of the world?" The disciples asked three questions. 1. When shall this happen? 2. When are You coming? 3. When is the end of the world? Matthew 24:4-5 "...and Jesus answered and said unto them, take heed that no man deceive you. For many shall come in My name, saying, 'I am Christ' and shall deceive many."

Growing up, I remember four distinct false prophets. 1. Osho or Rajneesh who changed his name to Bhagwan (god). He stated "if you've seen Jesus you have seen me, and if you've seen me you have seen Jesus." 2. Jonestown - Jim Jones, 3. Waco Texas - David Koresh, 4. Heaven's Gate - Marshall Applewhite, and there are a lot more. Matthew 24:6-7 "And you shall hear of wars and rumors of wars: see that you do not trouble yourself, for all these things must come to pass but the end is not yet: for nation shall rise against nation, and kingdoms against kingdoms: for there should be famines and pestilences and earthquakes in different places. All these are the beginning of sorrow."

Today nine countries together possess more than 16,000 nuclear weapons. The United States and Russia maintain roughly 1,800 of their nuclear weapons on high alert status ready to be launch within minutes of a warning. A single nuclear warhead, if detonated in a large city, could kill millions of people, with the effects persisting for decades. Here are the countries and their warheads: 1.United States 7,315 warheads, 2. Russia 8,000 warheads, 3. United Kingdom 225 warheads, 4. France 300 warheads, 5. China 250 warheads, 6. India 110 warheads, 7. Pakistan 120 warheads, 8. Israel 80 warheads, 9. North Korea 10 warheads. Total 16,400 warheads. Famine: the United Nations Food and Agriculture Organization estimates that nearly 870 million people of the 7.1 billion people in the world or one in eight, were suffering from chronic undernourishment 2010 – 2012. Almost all the hungry people, 852 million, live in developing countries. When I think about all the food that American's waste and leave on their plate's to throw in the garbage is very sad. In the Washington Post September 23, 2014 it says, "Americans throw out more food than plastic, paper, metals, and glass. In any article Waste by Weight in 2012 FOOD: says 34.7 million of tons, Plastic 28.9 m.t., Paper 24.4 m.t.,

Metal 14.8 m.t., Wood 13.4 m.t., Glass 8.4 m.t., Rubber 6.2 m.t., "Food waste is an incredible and absurd issue for the world today" José Lopez.

Pestilence: Seven Deadliest Diseases in History 1. Smallpox 2. Spanish 3. The Black Plague 4.Tuberculosis 5.Malaria 6.Ebola 7.Cholera. Earthquakes: Scientist Quake Expert; Earth is Cracking Up, 'Something is Seriously Wrong'. U.S. Geological Earthquakes Survey 1. Year 1974 – 4,528 Earthquakes, 2. Year 2000 – 19,131 Earthquakes, 3. Year 2010 – 23,040 Earthquakes, 4.Year 2011- 22,392 Earthquakes, 5.Year 2012 – 19,492 Earthquakes, 6. Year 2013 – 89,622 Earthquakes, In the first 9 months of 2014 – 89,324 Earthquakes. Matthew 24:9-10 "…then shall they deliver you up to be afflicted, and shall kill you: you shall be hated of all nations for My name's sake. And then shall many be offended, and shall betray one another, and shall hate one another. Jews and Christians right now are being persecuted and killed at an alarming rate today.

The world's watchlist unveiled the top 50 countries where the persecution of Christians is the worst. 1. North Korea, 2. Somalia, 3. Iraq, 4. Syria, 5. Afghanistan, 6. Sudan, 7. Iran, 8. Pakistan, 9. Eritrea, 10. Nigeria, etc. Matthew 24:12-13 "…and because iniquity shall abound, the love of many shall wax cold, but he that shall endure to the end the same shall be saved." No one *cannot* see lawlessness that pervades our society from the highest levels of government to the lowliest slum dwellers in our great cities. That is why none of us dare walk the city streets after dark, and many have heavily locked doors and put bars on their windows so they can sleep through the night. Schools and friends with liberal theology will persuade many to leave the faith. People will create new ways of sinning and tell you that it's okay and you should do it too. (Matthew 24:14 and this gospel of the kingdom shall be preached in all the world we are witnesses unto all nations; and then the end shall come). Gordon Condwell Center of the study of global Christianity calculates that Christians sent out approximately 400,000 international missionaries in 2010.

TECHTIMES says Google plans to send 180 satellites into orbit to improve global Internet access. Jesus said when the gospel was preached all around the world, and there is a number, and when that number is reached then the end will come. Romans 11:25 "…. Until the fullness of the Gentiles be come in." For almost 2000 years God has been warning and sending warnings, but mankind would not listen. Jeremiah 6:16-19 "Thus saith the Lord, Stand you in the ways, and see, and ask for the old paths, where is the good ways, and walk therein (do what I say), and you still find risks for your soul. But they say, we will not walk therein (not do what you say. Also I set watchmen over you, saying, hearken (listen to what I say) to the sound of the trumpet. But they say, we will not hearken. Therefore hear you nations, and know, O congregation, what is among them. Hear, O earth: behold, I will bring evil upon this people, even the fruit of their thoughts, because they are not hearkened unto my words, nor my laws, but rejected it."

God is the one that instituted marriage and marriage is between a man and a woman. But you tell God NO! I will do what I want to do!, And I will marry who I choose to marry. How then will you escape God's wrath? Please listen to God's voice and obey His laws before it's too late. Remember that God loves you and you are His creation.

Isaiah 9:15 "...that this is a rebellious people, lying children, children that will not hear the laws of the Lord: Which say to the watchmen, see not; and to the prophets, prophesy not unto us right things, speak unto us smooth things, prophesy deceits." I'm going to repeat this in layman terms: for if you don't write it, they will claim "I never heard them." "Oh, no," they'll say, "you never told us that" For they are stubborn rebels. They tell my servants, "Shut up"- we don't want any more of your reports!" Or they say, "Don't tell us the truth; tell us nice things; tell us lies. Forget all this gloom, we've heard more than enough about your 'Holy One of Israel' and all He says." But this is the reply of the Holy One of Israel, "Because you despise what I tell you and trust instead your friends and lies and won't repent, therefore calamity will come upon you suddenly, as upon a bulging wall that bursts and falls; in one moment it comes crashing down. God will smash you like a broken dish, He will not do it sparingly. Not a piece will be left large enough to use for carrying food from the stoves or a little water from the well. For the Lord God, the Holy One of Israel, says: only in returning to Me and waiting for Me will you be saved; and quietness and confidence shall be your strength, but you will have none of this. 'No,' you say. 'We will get our help from the world; they will give us swift tanks for riding into battle.' But the only swiftness you are going to see is the swiftness of your enemies chasing you! One of them will chase a thousand of you! Five of them will scatter you until not two of you are left together. You will be like lonely trees on a distant mountain top. Yet the Lord still wants for you to come to Him, so He can show you His love; He will conquer you to bless you, just as He said. For the Lord is faithful to His promises. Blessed are all those who wait for Him to help them."

Chapter 5

BLOOD MOONS

The Four Blood Moons

Before I get started, I would like to thank Mark Biltz, the man who discovered the blood moons. While on a trip to Israel on a feast day, he happened to notice a lunar eclipse, also called the blood moon in the sky over Jerusalem. He asked himself "I wonder if this happens more than once?". So he looked at NASA's website to find out more about the blood moon. To his surprise he found a certain pattern when the blood moons fall on Jewish feast days. If there are two blood moons in one year and there are two more blood moons on the next year they are called a tetrad. What's so amazing is he found out these tetrad's were very rare, especially when all of them fall on Jewish feast days.

Now let me explain what a blood moon and a solar eclipse is all about. A solar eclipse is when the sun is on one side, the earth is on the other side, and the moon is in the middle, and it lines up perfectly. A lunar eclipse, or blood moon, is when the sun is on one side, and the moon is on the other side, and the earth is in the middle, and it lines up perfectly. What makes the moon red is that when the sun hits the earth and reflects off the earth onto the moon, it turns it red.

The Talmud (Hebrew for study) is one of the central works of the Jewish people. It is a record of Rabbinic teachings that spanned a period of about 600 years beginning in the first century CE and continuing through the six and seventh century CE. The rabbinic teachings of the Talmud explain in great detail how the Commandments of the Torah are to be carried out. Talmud Sukkah 29A wrote: Our Rabbis taught, when the sun is in eclipse it is a bad omen for idolaters or when the sun is in eclipse, it is a bad omen for the whole world. When the moon is in eclipse, it is a bad omen for Israel. Since Israel reckons by the moon, then idolaters reckon by the sun. In summary, Lunar Eclipse = bad omen for the Jewish people in Israel; Blood Moon = sword coming; Solar Eclipse = bad omen for the world. For this to happen all will have to fall on Jewish feast days. The most solar eclipses you can have in one year is Seven (7), and a total solar eclipse lasts no more than Seven (7) minutes at any location on earth. There were Seven (7) Eclipses (4 eclipses of the sun; 3 of the moon the year General Allenby liberated Palestine from Turkish rule (Israel related) and the Balfour Decoration (concerning Jews returning to Israel).

In 1973 the Yom Kippur war (Six-Day War in Israel) there were Seven (7) Solar Eclipses that year. When Jesus died on the cross there was a blood moon and a solar eclipse. A series of 4 red Blood Moon lunar eclipses occurred on the Jewish Passover and the Feast of Tabernacles in 32 and 33 A.D. lunar. Jesus personally witnessed the first 2 lunar eclipses in 32 AD. Christ descended into Hell just prior to the Jewish Passover lunar eclipse in 33 A.D. having just been crucified only a few hours before, and had already ascended it to the Father in heaven by the time of the 33 A.D. feast of Tabernacles blood moon eclipses. Luke 23:44-46 "And it was about the sixth hour, and there was a darkness over all the earth until the ninth hour. In Wikipedia: Crucifixion darkness under Apocryphal: writers in a number of accounts in apocryphal literature built on the synoptic accounts of the crucifixion darkness. The Gospel of Peter, probably from the second century, on the canonical Gospel accounts of the passion narrative in creative ways. As some writers put it, accompanying miracles become more fabulous and the apocalyptic portents are more vivid." In this version, the darkness which covered the whole of Judea leads people to go about with lamps believing it to be night.

The fourth century gospel of Nicodemus describes how pilot and his wife were disturbed by a report of what had happened, and the Judeans he has summoned tell him it was an ordinary solar eclipse. Another text from the fourth century, the purported report of Pontius Pilate to Tiberius, claimed the darkness had started at the sixth hour, covered the whole world, and during the subsequent evening the full moon resembled blood the entire night – Pontius Pilate, 33 AD. In the fifth or sixth century texts by Pseudo-Dionysius the Areopagite, the author claims to have observed a solar eclipse from Heliopolis at the time of the crucifixion. Matthew 27:45, 27:51-54 "now from the sixth hour there was darkness over all the land until the ninth hour. And behold the veil of the temple was rent in twain from the top to the bottom; and the earth did quake, and the rocks rent, and the graves were open; and many bodies of the saints which slept arose, and came out of the graves after his resurrection, and went into the holy city, and a peer unto many. Now when the centurion, and they that were with him, watching Jesus, saw the earthquake, and those things which were done, they feared greatly, saying, truly this was the son of God." Blood Moon on Passover Apr 14, 32AD / Blood Moon on Tabernacle Oct. 07, 32AD / Crucifixion Jesus Christ Solar

Eclipse Apr 03, 33AD / Blood Moon on Passover Apr 03, 33AD / Blood Moon on Tabernacle Sep 27, 33AD. God said "and I will show you wonders in the heavens…" There were only eight tetrad's after Christ was on the cross. 1) 162-163 AD: Worst Persecution 2)795-796 AD: Islamic invasion 3)842-843 AD; Islamic invasion 4)860-861 AD: Islamic invasion 5)1493-1494. Jews Persecuted 6)1949-1950 Israel Re-established 7)1967-1968 Jerusalem Restored 8)2014-2015.

In 1948 Israel got their land back and there were 4 Blood Moons. In 1967 Israel got their capital back and there were 4 Blood Moons. In 2015 Israel will get their Temple back and there were 4 Blood Moons. **(Psalm 19:1-4 the heavens declare the glory of God, the sky proclaims the work of His hands. Day after day they pour forth speech, night after night they reveal knowledge, they have no speech, they use no words, no sound is heard from them, yet their voices go out to all the earth, their words to the ends of the world).**

Joel 2:31 "The sun shall turn into darkness, and the moon into blood, before the great and terrible day of the Lord comes." Acts 2:20 "The sun shall be turned into darkness, and the moon into blood, before that great and notable day of the Lord comes." Revelation 6:12 "And I beheld when He had opened the sixth seal, and, lo, there was a great earthquake; and the sun became black as sackcloth, and the moon became as blood; God said "The Sun will be in Eclipse and there will be a Blood Moon". This was said three times. The Blood Moon on, April 15, 2014 red total Lunar Eclipse that was seen in the United States on Passover lasted 77 minutes. The Blood Moon total lunar eclipse of September 28, 2015 will be a super red moon and be seen over Jerusalem. And there would not be another Tetrad on Jewish feast days for another 500 years. Remember that a blood Moon and a solar eclipse on Jewish feast day always brings war but then out of war comes peace and fulfillment. Never since Christ was on the cross till today 2015 have we had 4 Blood Moons and 2 Solar Eclipses on Jewish feast days fall in a Tetrad. War is coming are you ready? Out of all the blood moons in the solar eclipses there has never been one like this one, this solar eclipse is the only one that falls on Rosh Hashanah, the Feast of Trumpets or Yom Teruah. Rosh Hashanah is on September 13, 2015 on a Sunday, the first day of the week. Rosh Hashanah is a Jewish idiom for "no one knows the day or the hour". The solar eclipse that falls on Rosh Hashanah has never happened before and will never happen again.

Go to www.DoublePortionInheritance.com, look at (PICTURE 2) read Yom Teruw'ah: "The Day that No Man Knows" by Maria Merola . On Rosh Hashanah, a series of 100 trumpet blasts is sounded to announce the setting up of the eternal court, heralding God as the All Seeing, All-Knowing Judge over the universe. The 100 shofar blasts signifies that heaven gates are open wide with the King seated upon the Throne. His scepter of grace and mercy are extended in a special way at this time and all throughout the next 10 days. Jewish tradition says that this court date is to find out who are the righteous and have their names in the Book of Life. All other people are a mixture of good and bad, and God in His mercy will delay their court date for a period of a time to allow them to try and prepare a proper defense. The second court date is on Yom Kippur. After 99 blasts of the shofar, the final 100th blast is the loudest and the longest. It is called Tekiah

Gedolah. I believe this trumpet sound is the one signified in 1 Thessalonians 4:16. "For the Lord Himself will descend from heaven with a shout, with the voice of an archangel, and with the (Tekiah Gedolah) trumpet of God: and the dead in Christ will rise first".... Acts 17:11 tells us "Now the Bereans were of more notable character than the Thessalonians, for they received the message with great eagerness and examined the Scriptures every day to see if what Paul said was true."

Signs in the Sun, Moon and the Stars

The sun, moon and stars were originally created by the Almighty to draw universal attention to the spectacular deeds He planned to perform on the appointed Feast Days, seasons and sabbatical years in the sacred calendar. This astonishing fact is mentioned in the very first chapter of the Bible. Genesis 1:14 says: "And God said, let there be light in the firmament of the heavens to divide the day from the night; and let them be for signs, and for seasons, and for days, and years": according to the Strong's Bible dictionary: the Hebrew word owth (oth) translated 'sign' in this verse means: a signal, distinguishing mark, banner, remembrance, miraculous sign, omen, warning. And the Hebrew word mow'ed (mo-ade) translated 'seasons' in this verse means: appointed place, appointed time, appointed meeting, sacred season, set feast, tent of meeting. In other words: the sun and the moon were set in the heavens to signal the appointed sacred seasons, the set feast, when Israel was together and worship at the creators tent of meeting. To be sure the sun and the moon determine the literal days, nights, seasons and years and they directly influence the climate. But the language of

Genesis 1:14 goes far beyond these natural events. It tells of the spiritual reasons why the sun and moon were created. To serve as celestial warning signs and omens to signal the sacred seasons, feast days and years of the Almighty God. They were placed in the sky by the Most High to alert the universe of His appointed meeting times; when the human race is called to worship Him. Bible prophecies confirm the message of Genesis 1:14 by telling us that just before Jesus Christ's return to earth there will be "signs in the sun and the moon"

Extra Extra read all about it!

"The Bible is still relevant for today and is more up-to-date then tomorrow's newspaper. Biblical prophecy stands as a stark warning to unbelievers that God's fingerprints are all over the Bible. The word Prophecy is found in the Bible 21 (777) times. The Bible is written in three parts, salvation, history and prophecy. Salvation tells us how God redeemed His people, history teaches His people what to do and what not to do, and prophecy teaches His people that God keeps His promises. I have heard it said that prophecy is one of the strongest proofs pointing to the fact that the Bible is from God. Various books cite different figures, depending upon the manner of which one counts prophecies. For example, one writer may count a single verse as a prophecy, while others may see three or four prophetic elements within the same passage. One thing I know for sure is that the God of the Bible has fulfilled every prophecy in the past and up to the present to the letter, and He will regarding the ones for the future as well. There is no person and not one book ever written that can do that. Some people say "I see God doing stuff back then but what is He doing today?" God is the same yesterday, today, and forever.

Remember we talked about God's signature the number seven (7), (77), (777), let's look at how He signs His name on everything again and again. We discussed earlier about the 9/11 attack; it was seven buildings that were destroyed. 1. The South Tower, 2. The North Tower, 3. Southeast Plaza building, 4. Northeast Plaza building, 5. U.S. Customhouse, 6. Marriott Hotel, 7. Solomon Brothers building. There are a lot of conspiracy theorists and structural engineers saying "in my judgment fires did not bring down World Trade Center building seven (7)." You see World Trade Center seven was across the street from all the other buildings. They could not figure out how this building collapsed. So they protested and said "World trade building seven just didn't blow itself up". What's so interesting is about World Trade Center Seven (7) is that it fell down seven (7) hours later. Also another interesting fact is that, Ronald H Buchman, a structural engineer, with a master degree in engineering from UC Davis writes: why would all 47 stories of World Trade Center seven fall straight down to the ground in about Seven (7) seconds the same day. The seventh building, the seventh hour, seven seconds, 777. On the Jewish calendar it would have been the seventh month.

Do you know after all the debris and all the twisted metal they found a Cross at Ground Zero. God was saying "I was there and I allowed this to happen to America". I want them to repent before it's too late". This question was asked to Billy Graham: Q: Does God still judge nations for their sins, like He did in the Old Testament times? And if so, how bad does a nation have to get before God will finally give up on it and bring down judgment upon it? A: Yes, God still judges nations for their sins -- just as He still judges us as individuals. The Bible is clear: "You may be sure that your sins will find you out" (Numbers 32:23). After all, God hasn't changed over the centuries; He is holy and pure, and whenever we scorn Him, we run the risk of incurring His judgment. Sin is an offense to Him - and the reason is because sin is a deliberate denial of God and His will for our lives. When we sin, we deliberately turned our backs on God and say our way is better than His. But we are wrong - and eventually we will pay the price. The Bible warns that "the wages of sin is death" (Romans 6:23). The same is true of a nation that rejects God. When ancient Israel turned against God, the prophets warned that God's judgment would eventually come upon them - and it did. But God also warned that the surrounding nations would be judged too because they had no regards for God- and they were. Sometimes it happens in one great catastrophe; sometimes it happens in a series of smaller disasters and defeats. But it happens.

Jonathan Cahn's book The Harbinger tackles a lot of these questions. He talks about how the World Trade Center was conceived in 1945, a Shemitah Year and how Isaiah 9:10-11 was prophetic. He talked about how America is following the same path that Israel did and America is headed for judgment. (Isaiah 9:8-10 to Isaiah 9:11 "The Lord sent a word into Jacob, and it had lighted upon Israel. And all the people shall know, even Ephraim and its inhabitants of Samaria, that say in the pride and stoutness of their heart... The bricks are fallen, but we will build with hewn stones; the sycamores are cut down, but we will change them to Cedar"). On 911 the bricks came falling down and in the process of rebuilding America they brought in a great hewn stone. Isaiah said that the Sycamore was cut down. On 9/11 one of the beams from the twin towers fell and cut down a sycamore tree. Isaiah said we should change it to a Cedar tree, so after 9/11 they replaced a sycamore tree with a cedar tree. And they also built a monument at Ground Zero called St. Paul's church sycamore stump.

Tom Daschle's speech on September 12, 2001 was the very next day. I have to remind you that Tom Daschle did not go to New York on or the day after 9/11, so he would've known all of the intricate details that happened there, but quoted Isaiah 9:10. In Hebrew Cedar means strength and purity: (Leviticus 14:49 "To cleanse the house then, he shall take two birds and Cedar wood and a scarlet string and hyssop,") it was called the tree of hope and the tree of hope did not prosper and eventually withered away. The tipping point came when on the day of Passover of the blood Moon April 15, 2014, the tree was unceremoniously uprooted and destroyed. This symbol of purity could not take root in poor soil! Why did this tree of hope die? I believe that God is trying to send a message to the world literally, prophetically, and spiritually. That message is that even though this was a tree of hope there is no hope without Christ. The Hebrew translation of Shemitah is "To Release". The Shemitah years were meant to be a blessing for God's people. As soon as the early Jews settled in the Holy Land, they began to observe the seven year cycle. But they fell away from God and ignored the seven-year Sabbaths before hundred 490 years. Soon the blessings of Shemiteh turned to judgment. In 586 BC, the nation of Israel was destroyed. The Temple was devastated, the land burned, and the people were taken captive to Babylon, where they stayed and waited for 70 years. Why 70 years? To repay the 70 Shemiteh years they had failed to observe for 490 years. The land was given and enforced rests until their return. The principal of Shemiteh had determined the timing of judgment. (Our Father has told us everything through His word, surely the Lord God will do nothing, but He revealeth His secrets unto His servants the prophets Amos 3:7). "But take ye heed: behold, I have foretold you all things." Mark 13:23.

There's a man who went to the doctor and he told the doctor that he had a hearing problem. So the doctor took out his watch and he asked the man "can you hear this?'. And the man replied "yes". So the doctor walked away several feet and asked the man again "can you hear this?" And the man replied again "yes" so the doctor walked away a total of 7 feet and asked the man "can you hear this? And the man said again "yes" the doctor said to the man you don't have a hearing problem you have a listening problem! Learn to listen to God.

God's final warning to America is being spoken forth and we are approaching the final climax of Western history. The stock market has been crashing every seven years since 1966. Now if we simply looked at the seven year periods from 1966, I get 1973, 1980, 1987, 1994, 2001, 2008, 2015. Seven (7) Sabbatical year cycles and then the 7 X 7 cycles of the Yovel. There is a seventh year cycle and a related 50 year cycle in the Jewish calendar. The Shemitah Year, the sabbatical Year, is each Seven (7th) Years, / and the Yovel, the Jubilee Year, is each fiftieth (50th) Year. The Yovel is the Fiftieth (50th) year; it occurs the year after the Seven cycles of the Seven years. With regards to agriculture, it is treated as a Schmidt year. Cycle will look like this example: 41-(42)-43-44-45-46-47-48-(49)-(((50)))-

51-52-53-54-55-(56)-57-58-59-60-61-62-(63)-64-65-66-67-68-69-(70)-71-72- so the 50 also counted as one and 51 counted as two and 56 counted as seven and 57 counted as one and 58 counts as two and 63 counts as seven: so the whole 49 through 50 is Yovel. 1. All slaves were to be set free in the Yovel Year. A biblical inscription to this effect was inscribed by the founding fathers of the United States of America on the Liberty Bell, which is now displayed in Philadelphia. The text reads, "And thou shall proclaim liberty in the land of all its inhabitants." (Leviticus 25,10).

Incidentally, many of the founding fathers were quite familiar with the Hebrew Bible and, according to one account, actually considered adopting Hebrew as a national language. 2. All sales of the land will return to the original owner in the Fiftieth (50th) year. Thus, there were only leases of property for periods up to 49 years there were no sales "in perpetuity" of parcels of land in the land of Israel. "For the land is mine; you are only temporarily residence and sellers together with Me. This picture shows every seven years, and when you get to the 49th year is starts 1 all over again but we counted 50. This is only for the 49th and thru 50th year. The 51st years will be counted as 2 and 56th we count as 7. The Yovel starts at the end of the 49th year or at end of Shemitah and goes on to the ends of the 51st at the start of the 52nd year. (lev 25, 23)". 1/7 @ 2/14 @ 3/21 @ 4/28 @ 5/35 @ 6/42 @ 7/49 to 1/50 - 2\51 – 52 – 53 – 54 – 55 – 7\56 @ 2/63 @ 3/70 @ 4/77 etc. another example how you count the 50 is one.

On September 17, 2001 on a Monday the stock market crashed and the Dow Jones dropped almost 7 points at 7%. And on September 29, 2008 on a Monday the stock market crashed and the Dow Jones drops 777 points as 7%. Seven years later September 13, 2015? Remember Jesus was a Jew, you won't find January, February, March, April etc. in the Bible. But what you will find is the Jewish months in the Bible, Nisan, Iyar, Sivan, Tammuz, etc. Tishri is the seventh month on the Jewish calendar, the middle of September to the middle of October. When the stock market crashed September 17, 2001, that was on Rosh Hashanah. When the stock market crashed in September 29, 2008, that was on Rosh Hashanah. Ten days later is Yom Kippur October 9, 2008, and the Dow tumbles 7% on that day. Five days later is Sukkot or Feast of Tabernacles October 15, 2008, another huge Dow loss at 7 points.

On Monday, September 29, 2008, the Congress of the United States was meeting and what was to be one of the most important historical sessions in history not only for America, Wall Street, but also the rest of the world. As the Jewish congressmen were pushing for a roll call so that they would exit and fly back to their hometown to celebrate Rosh Hashanah the Jewish New Year, the House of Representatives rejected the US700 Billion Dollar rescue plan to bail out the financial industry. It's was called the 700 Billion Emergency Economic Stabilization Plan or (BAILOUT) in order to prevent what is heralded as a widespread financial collapse. In a vote of 228 – 205 a bi-partisan vote including 133 Republicans to 95 Democrats congressmen opposing the bill that same day the United States stock market plummeted on an average of 777 points. Jim Richards: the Financial Threat and Asymmetric Warfare Advisor to both the Pentagon and the CIA says "We're on the verge of entering the darkness economic period in our National history". He wrote a book called THE DAY AFTER PLAN.

Donald Trump: tells Americans to prepare for "financial ruins". Billionaire Jeremy Grantham: warns that an horrific stock market crash is coming. Janet Yellen says the collapse will be unlike any other. Pope Francis warns the global economy is near collapse. Forbes Magazine tells why the next financial crisis could be worse than 2008.

What if you don't make the rapture? One day you are going to wake up to a shocking revelation. News Headline Sunday Morning New York Post September 13, 2015 the Dow Jones Crashes down to 70% and the dollar is worthless. The banks are closed and The World Bank has collapsed. What would you do? How would you survive? Well, first America will be in chaos, riots and looting everywhere in the street. Marshal Law will go into effect to restore law and order. America's debt is at 18 trillion dollars and rising and America can't pay the interest. Do you know why the media is so quiet, if they told you your money will be worthless in a week what would you do? You and 300 million Americans would run to the bank and demand your money. Time is running out, don't put your trust in the government, man, family, friends, put your trust in God. Learn from history, take your head out of the sand and look around and just because you won't look does it mean it won't happen.

Chapter 6

THE BOOK OF DANIEL NOW OPEN
(Daniel 12:4)

The book of Daniel

The Bible is full of literal, figurative, symbolic, "Types and Shadows". The book of Daniel is written in two sections: chapters one through six are miracles, and seven through twelve are prophecy. One through six is about him during Babylon. Seven through twelve is about Daniel = I, by Him, after or future. One through six has six chapters, and the first chapter was written in Hebrew, and the next five chapters were written in Aramaic. Seven through Twelve has six chapters, and the first chapter was written in Aramaic in the next five chapters written in Hebrew. I want to deal with seven through Twelve of Daniel's prophecy and the future events. When looking through the eyes of Daniel it is like looking through a telescope: you see two mountain peaks, one in the front and one in the back.

One mountain peak is the First Coming and the other mountain peak is the Second Coming. Between the two mountain peaks there is a valley and Daniel cannot see the valley. Daniel could see all the way up to the time of Christ, but then could not see the valley, he could only see the last part of world history. Daniel 9:24-27 "Seventy weeks (490 years) are determined upon by people and upon thy holy city, to finish the transgressions, and to make eight of sin, and to make reconciliation for iniquity, and to bring in everlasting righteousness, and to seal up the vision and prophecies, and to account the most holy. Know therefore and understand, that from the going forth of the Commandments to restore and build Jerusalem onto the Messiah the Prince shall be seven weeks, and three scores and two weeks (483 years) ; the street shall be built again, and the wall, even in troubled times. And after three score and two weeks shall Messiah be cut off (killed), (First Mountain Peak) but not for himself; (Second Mountain Peak) and the people of the Prince (antichrist) that shall come shall destroy the city and the sanctuary; and the end thereof shall be with a flood and into that and of the war desolate are determined. And he (antichrist) shall confirm the covenant with many for one week (7 years); and in the midst of the week he shall cause the sacrifices and the oblation to cease and for the off spreading of abominations he shall make it desolate, even until the consummation, and that determined shall be poured up on the desolate."

Notice between the two mountain peaks there is a valley that Daniel cannot see. Daniel could not see most of the 2000 years of grace period. He only could see the last seven years of world history. There is a mistake that a lot of people make, they tried to add the first part of Daniel to the second part of Daniel. The mistake is Nebuchadnezzar had a dream in the first part, and in the second part Daniel had a dream. Let's look at Daniel's dream; Daniel 7:1 -- In the first year of Belshazzar King of Babylon, Daniel had a dream and vision and he wrote it down. This is the description of what he saw: "Then you spake and said I saw in my vision by night, and, behold, the four winds of the heavens shove upon the great sea. And four great beasts came up from the seat different from one another.

The First Beast was like a lion; and has Eagle wings (Britain and America). I beheld the wings thereof were plucked (America left Britain), and it lifted up from the earth, and made staying up on the feet as a man (Uncle Sam), and a man's heart was given to it (the heart of America) or (America is born). And I beheld another Second Beast, like unto a Bear (Russia), and it raised up itself on one side, it had three ribs in his mouth and between his teeth (Winston Churchill, Franklin D Roosevelt and Joseph Stalin). And they said thus into it, arise devour much flesh (World War 2). After this I beheld and lo, another Third Beast, like a leopard (European Union), which had upon his back of it four wings of a fowl (states birds), the beast had also four heads, and dominion was given to it. After this I saw in the night vision and behold a Fourth Beast (United Nations), dreadful and terrible, and strong exceedingly, and it had great iron teeth: it devoured and break in pieces and stamp the residue with the feet of it. And it was diverse (more brutal than any of the others) from all the beasts that were before it; and it had 10 horns. Revelation 13:2 "...and the Fourth Beast which I saw was like into a leopard (European Union) and his feet were as the feet of a bear (Russia) in his mouth as the mouth of a lion (Britain and America) and the dragon gave him power in his seat and great authority." (all are in the United Nations). Daniel 7:17 "...these Great Beasts, which are four, are four kings, which shall arise out of the earth.... Then I would know the truth of the fourth beast which was diverse (more brutal than any of the others) from all the others, exceedingly dreadful, whose teeth were iron, and his nails of brass, which divide and break into pieces and stepped residue with his feet." Daniel 7:23 "Thus he said, The Fourth Beast (United Nations), shall be the fourth kingdom upon the earth, will shall be diverse (more brutal than any of the others) for all the kingdoms and shall devour the whole earth and shall tear it down and break it in pieces."

Now let's take a look at the fourth beast of Daniel. Remember I said the Bible is like a big newspaper, man writes history *after* it happens, but God writes it *before* it happens. Listen to this, and look at the line about Eagle wings. The Lion is Britain, why? Google: what country has a Lion as a national symbol? United Kingdom. Their symbol is a Lion. Let's look at the Eagle wings. Google: Eagle is a national symbol of which country? USA. Remember the Spanish Inquisition the year 1492 where the Roman Catholic Church told the Jews to convert to Catholicism or die or leave Spain? Well, a Jew by the name of Christopher Columbus found the Jews a new home which happen to be America. Christopher Columbus found the Jews America, where there are more Jews here than anywhere in the world except Israel. The Jews were evicted from Spain on the 9th of AV, a Jewish holiday of morning falling on 1 August 1492. Shortly thereafter a series of four total lunar eclipses occurred during the Spanish Inquisition on God/Jewish Feast Days. For Blood Moons on 1. April 2 1493 Passover, 2. September 25 1493 Feast of Trumpets, 3. March 22 1494 Passover, 4. September 15 1494 Feast of Trumpets. Two blood moons on Nisan 14, and two blood moons on Tishri 15.

Google: Early American Jews from Inquisition to freedom. There are 13 stars above the Eagle. He is on a dollar bill that shapes the Star of David. Daniel said that the wings were plucked and it was lifted from the earth (traveling by boat to the Americas), and made to stand on his feet as a man (you just realized Uncle Sam's initials are U.S.), and a man's heart would get into it (Heart of America or Heart-

Land).

The American Revolution war began on April 19, 1775 as a war between the kingdom of Great Britain and the 13 British colonies in North America. Let's look at Daniel's vision of the next beast which is the BEAR. Google: Bear is a national symbol of what country? Russia. Russia has two Russian nuclear capable "Bear" bombers. A more interesting article says that Russia analysis of grades to nuclear arsenal with new "Satan" ICBM or Intercontinental ballistic missile in 2012. But today's news, Russia is to create a "Son of Satan" missile to be deployed in 2018.

Let's look at Daniel's third beast which is the Leopard. Google; the Leopard is a national symbol of which country? Germany/European Union. The Economist magazine article of December 10, 2009 says lessons from "The Leopard" Europe. News headline: Berlin approves huge tank deal with Indonesia "the Leopard 2 tanks are in demand around the world. News article "the European Union's Mediterranean policies after the air springs: Can a Leopard change its Spots? Another headline reads "You must stick with austerity"; the austerity Leopard will not change its spots.

The Fourth Beast and the Last Beast is more terrible than them all. Revelations 13:2 describes this beast which looks like a Leopard, has the feet of a Bear, and the mouth of a Lion. The fourth beast of Daniel 7 merged into one beast in Revelation 13, all three in one. Daniel 7:7 ..... "And it was diverse (more brutal than any of the others) from all the beasts that were before it; it had 10 horns." (Ten Kings). The United Nations is the Fourth and Dreadful Beast and is made up of all the countries with membership of 193 member states. At its founding, the United Nations had 51 member states; there are now 193, "...who can make war with him." – Revelation 13:4.

Extra! Extra! read all about it March 10, 2012 "Middle East Quartet to meet next week." "The quartet of the Middle East which includes Russia, the United States, the European Union and the United Nations, will hold his next meetings on Monday. The quartet includes 1.Britain, United States 2.Russia, 3.United Nations and the 4. European Union. God writes history before it happens. "The 10 horns which thou saw are 10 kings" – Revelation 17:12. The 10 kings are called the "Berlin Club" and are comprised of 1. Belgium, 2. France, 4.Germany, 4. Greece, 5. Italy, 6. Luxembourg, 7. Netherlands, 8. Portugal, 9. Spain, and 10. United Kingdom. The Berlin Club use to be called the Western European Union. The Western European Union grew until it was ten nations in 1995. These 10 nations all are members of the EU European Union and reside in the territories that at different times in history of the Roman Empire were part of the Empire. Revelation 13:3 "...and I saw one of his heads as it were wounded to death, and the deadly wound was healed: and all the world wondered after the beasts."

A lot of people read this Scripture and say antichrists will be shot in the head or there will be an attempt assassination. But if you read very carefully it says "One of his Heads" so if he has 10 heads, it's only one head was wounded to death. That head is Germany. Germany has plunged Europe into war three times within 70 years, 1. Francisco Germany war 1870, 2. World War I, 3. World War II. To ensure that this would never happen again, the Allies and Russia decided to divide Germany, half going to the East and half going to the West. They built a wall straight through Germany and it was called "The Berlin Wall". Germany was split: the East and the West. The East went to Russia and the West went to the United States, Britain and France.

Extra! Extra! read all about it: USA Today Magazine in 1986 describes the Berlin Wall as   "The 29˙-mile wound that wouldn't heal." George Ball, the seventh United States Ambassador to the UN made this statement : "In terms of oral policies, the most dangerous of these problems is the division of Europe, which means the division of Germany. This division that festers like a rusty knife must someday be healed. The Berlin wall was built and opened in 1961 and it was torn down in 1989. For 28 years the deadly wound was healed, and the two countries were reunited into one Germany, when Mikhail Gorbachev ordered the Berlin wall torn down in 1998." Extra! Extra! Read all about it: Time Magazine Monday, November 20, 1998 Hall of shame 1961-1989 says "It was the most palpable evidence of a deep wound in European civilization -- and it is finally gone." On June 12, 1987 President Ronald Reagan delivered a speech in front of the Berlin iconic Brandenburg Gate in which he memorably demands; "Mr. Gorbachev, tear down this Wall!" On November 9, 1998 the whole world watched in amazement as jubilant crowds gathered on both sides of the Berlin Wall around midnight to celebrate the opening of the border crossing between the Eastern and Western parts of the city. (Revelation 13:3 ..... And all the world wondered after the beast). It inspired all globalists and the United Nations in international affairs to take a giant leap towards world government.

Let's look back at Daniel 2:38-42 where he interprets Nebuchadnezzar's dream, "Nebuchadnezzar, you Babylon are the head of gold, and after you – arise in the kingdom (Silver the Medo-Persian Empire) inferior to you, and another third kingdom of Brass (Alexander the Great), which shall be a rule over all the earth. And the fourth kingdom shall be strong as Iron (The Roman Empire): for as much as iron breaks it in pieces and subdues under it all things: and as iron that breaketh all these, shall he break in pieces and bruise (Romans not destroyed, it disintegrated). And where you saw the feet and the toes, part of potter's clay, and part of Iron. (Could this be church and state? Clay = Church and Iron = State). The kingdom shall be divided, but there shall be in it of the strengths of the iron, much as you see it the iron mix with miry (dirty) Clay (Clay always changes form into whatever you like). And as the toes of the feet were part iron, and part of clay, so the kingdom shall be partly strong and partly broken." (Catholicism always changes like the Clay). It tries to mingle itself in every religion of the world. We know that this last kingdom will rule the world at the time of Christ's return.

The Bible tells us that will have two Beasts, a Political leader and a Religious leader. Revelation 13:11 "…and I beheld another beast (1 more beast) coming out of the earth: and it had two horns like a lamb, and he spake like a dragon (looks like a Christian but speaks like the devil).

Extra! Extra! Read all about it: Pope Francis says "All can go to Heaven, even Atheists". Pope Francis tries to look like a Christian, but speaks like the devil. Extra! Extra! Read all about it: Pope Francis says "You don't have to believe in God to go to heaven" but the Bible says unless a man is born again he can never see God. Born-again is in the Bible three times. Pope Benedict has announced that his faithful can once again pay the Catholic Church to ease their way through purgatory and get into the gates of heaven or by your way to heaven. Extra! Extra! Read all about it: Lightning struck St. Peter's Basilica Monday, hours after Pope Benedict XVI announced that he will resign as leader of the world's 1.1 Billion Catholics on February 28.

Never mind that Martin Luther fired up the Reformation because of them. In order to appease the world Catholicism embraces all kinds of pagan practices of the Roman empire to gain converts. Many include 1.) Found the church and apostle Peter rather than and Christ Jesus alone - 1 Corinthians 10:4, 2.) Claimed/claim to be God's owner, in that the Pope can modify God's divine law – Dan 7:25, 3.) Pope and priest are called "father" in a spiritual sense while Jesus condemns this – Matthew 23:9, 4.) Ordain infant baptism which is nowhere in the Bible, 5.) Forbid marriage of priest and nuns – 1 Timothy 4:2-3, practice repetitive prayer (Hail Mary), 6.) Brought in pagan practices like Easter, Good Friday, Palm Sunday etc. Revelation 13:12 "…and he exercise all the power of the first beast before him, and causes the earth and them that dwell therein to worship (the second beast made them worship the first beast) the first beast, whose deadly wound was healed."

In Daniel let's look at some of the symbolism of the revived Roman Empire. (Picture 4) Caesar wore a golden laurel wreath around his head, in Rome they wear symbols of martial victory, crowning a successful commander during his triumph. In Greek mythology, Apollo is represented with a laurel wreath on his head. In ancient Greece wreaths were awarded to victors, athletic competitions, including the ancient Olympics made of wild olive tree known as "kotinos". This was used in the old Roman Empire. Today this symbol has resurfaced to the new Roman Empire. The United Nations uses this symbol "Laurel wreath" as their nation's symbol. Google: SPQR and Google United Nations and look at their symbols.

On March 25,1957 the Treaty of Rome was set up establishing the European Economic Community. Two treaties were signed on March 25, 1957: the treaty establishing the European Economic Community EEC and the treaty establishing the European Atomic Energy Community EAEC. The European Parliamentary assembly held its first session the following year on March 19, 1958. The assembly increased in size to 142 members. With the Treaty of Rome, a specific provision is made for members to be directly elected. After World War II, Monnet was the second most powerful man in France. Frenchman Jean Monnet first begin to dream of building a "United States of Europe". Treaty by treaty, it would take over more power from national governments, based on a sacred principle that once power to make law is handed over to Brussels it could never be given back. More countries will be brought into the net, until the project's ultimate goal as a super government, with its own president and parliament, its own currency and Armed Forces, its own flag and national anthem and then a new world order. You see the Treaty of Rome is well on its way and no one can stop it.

Extra! Extra! Read all about it: "We want a United States of Europe says top EU official". Paul-Henri Spaak, one of the founding fathers of the (EEC) European Economic Communities said "**What we want is a man of sufficient stature to hold the allegiance of all people and to lift us out of the economic morass into which we are sinking.**

Send us such a man, and be he god or devil, we will receive him."

Extra! Extra! Read all about it: the new international criminal Court or Rome Statute of the International Criminal Court (where world kings can be punished). Today we call this " The New World Order". A lot of world leaders today are calling for a new world order. President Obama is calling for New World order, vice president Joe Biden says "The affirmative tasks we have now will actually create a new world order", former president George Bush senior says "it is a big idea: a new world order... Only the United States has both the moral standings and the means to back it up", Mikhail Gorbachev says "We had 10 years after the Cold War to build a new world order and yet we squandered them. The United States cannot tolerate anyone acting independently".

Henry Kissinger says "Obama's task is to help create a new world order". George Herbert Walker Bush says the war in Iraq is a rare opportunity to move towards an historic period of cooperation. Out of these troubled times... A new world order can emerge".

James Warburg, member of the Council on foreign relations says "We shall have world government whether or not you like, by conquests or consent". Arthur Schlesinger, Jr in foreign affairs says "We are not going to achieve a new world order without paying for it in blood as well as in word and money". David Rockefeller from his own book Memoirs page 405 states "Some even believe we are part of a secret cabal working against the best interests of the United States, characterizing my family and me as internationalists and of conspiring with others around the world to build a more integrated global political and economic structure - one world, if you will. If that's the charge, I stand guilty, and I am proud of it." Daniel talks about a one world leader that will sign a treaty that will last seven years. Daniel 9:27 "...and he shall confirm a covenant with many for one week (7 years) and in the midst (middle) of the week (7 years) he shall cause the sacrifice (animal sacrifice) and the oblation to cease and of the overspreading of abominations you shall make it desolate, even until the consummation, and that determined shall be poured out upon the desolate."

Let me ask you a question if the tribulation period lasts seven years, how long will the antichrist be upon the earth? If you answered seven years you are correct. My next question is will we see the antichrist? 2 Thessalonians 2:3-8 says "Let no man deceive you by any means: for that day shall not come except there be a falling away first and the man of sin be revealed the son of perdition (The Antichrist) who opposes and exalts himself above all that is called God, or that is worshiped; so that he as making himself like God will sit in the temple (the third temple not built yet) of God showing himself that he is God. Remember when I was with you and I told you these things? And you know what withholds him (antichrist) that he (antichrist) may be revealed at this time. For the mystery of iniquity (sin) does already work: only he who now letteth will let (but he himself will not come to the one who is holding them back steps out of the way), until he (Holy Spirit) be taken out of the way. And then shall the wicked one be revealed, whom the Lord shall consume with the spirit of His mouth, and shall destroy with the brightness of His coming (God's coming back to earth, the second coming)." You see the antichrist will rule for seven years and God says that the Holy Spirit is holding him back, and once the Holy Spirit is taken out of the way only then can he be revealed.

God put Noah and his family on the ark but left the door open for seven more days (symbolizing the tribulation period). God gave man seven more days to repent and get on the ark, and God again will give man seven more years to repent and make it to heaven, but this time you will pay with your life. Isaiah 26:19-21 "Thy dead man shall live, together with my dead bodies shall they arise, Awake and saying, you that dwell in the dust: for your dew is as the dew of herbs, and the earth shall cast out the dead. Come, My people, enter thou into the chambers (wedding chambers), and shut thy door about thee (shut the door behind you): hide thyself as it were a little moment (7 years), until the indignation (anger and punishment) be over past (has passed). For behold, the Lord, out of His place (as a roaring Lion) comes to punish the inhabitants of the earth for their iniquity: the earth also shall disclose her blood and shall no more cover her stain (my blood shall no longer cover her (world) sins)."

When Jews got married in Bible days the bride kept her veil over her face as she entered the bridal chamber and only after seven days was she allowed to show her face. The wedding party, immediately after the wedding, would party for seven days and would not see the bride's face until after the seven days. Once the rapture of the Church takes place, Jesus will take His Bride, His followers, the believers, and we will go away for seven years and after the seven years only then will the world get to see the Bride. 1 Thessalonians 3:13 "....At the coming of our Lord Jesus Christ with all his saints." The Jewish term for this day is "Ha Kiddushin", the wedding day of the Messiah.

The whole Bible is like a big Jewish wedding. Bride is in the Bible Fourteen (14) times and Wedding is in the Bible Seven (7) times (14+7) or (777) or (21). God is the one that instituted marriage between a man and a woman. Genesis 2:18, 24 "For the Lord God said it is not good for man to be alone. I will make a helper suitable for him." Verse 24 says "...that is why man leaves his father and his mother and his united to his wife, and they become one flesh."

Hebrew wedding customs have prophetic significance and will display fulfillment in the last days. 1. The bridegroom's father makes and approves the choice of the bride – John 10:29. When a Jew asks his girlfriend to marry him and she says "yes" he says "I'm going away to prepare a place for us" who said that? Jesus. So when the Jewish man sees his father and tells him that I found a bride, the father says let's start working on your home. In a Jewish wedding invitations are never given out, so when someone was see you they would ask "when are you getting married? The next thing you would say "I don't know! But my father knows. So when the houses finish the father would tell his son he can go get his bride. As a son goes in town to get his bride they would blow a trumpet and shout "the bridegroom is coming! The bridegroom is coming! Once the bridegroom gets his bride and they get married under the Chuppah, they take off for seven days. The party is still going on for seven days while the bride and groom are in the marriage chamber. After the seven days are finished the bride and groom emerge from the marriage chamber and revealed themselves as wedded husband and wife to the whole world.

Let's look at it in God's eyes: God asked us to marry Him and we say? Yes or no. If the answer is yes we will put on an engagement ring, and the bride would run and show the world she's engaged. But God will give us His engagement ring "the Holy Spirit" and we want to continue to run after the ways of the world.? As the bride is waiting patiently for the big day of the marriage, we are waiting patiently for that big day where we will marry Christ forever. Because He is gone away to prepare a place for us that where He is we may be there also – John 14:3.

The Book of Revelation speaks of a great marriage supper of the Lamb in which the bride will be joined with Christ. Revelation 19:7-9 "Let us be glad and rejoice and give him glory, for the marriage of the Lamb has come, and His Bride has made herself ready. And to her it was granted to be arrayed in fine linen, clean and bright, for the fine linen is the righteous acts of the saints. Then He said to me, Write: 'Blessed are those who are called to the marriage supper of the Lamb!'"

We will understand the nature of the marriage ceremony more fully when we have a better understanding of the Jewish marriage customs upon which it is modeled. When understanding the Jewish wedding and the feast of Tabernacles, will be able to gather some thoughts concerning this event. The first day of Tishrei is Rosh Hashanah, a two-day event following 10 days to Yom Kippur, they are therefore known as the "Ten Days of Awe." These 10 days are devoted to self-examination and repentance from one sin in preparation for judgment on Yom Kippur, the Day of Atonement. These Ten days of Awe are a type of "day of trouble" (Jeremiah 30:7) that is to come before the second coming of the Messiah. Today Christians call this the tribulation period. I believe the seven years are the week (seven days) before the marriage supper. Before you can have a wedding, all the saints or brides would have to be there. All the martyrs, all the rapture Saints, and all the tribulation saints will have to be at the wedding. Yom Kippur is the day Jesus will atone and redeem His Bride fully. This is the day Jesus will physically return to earth. The Bible clearly states Jesus will return immediately after the Great Tribulation. Matthew 24:29 "...Immediately after the Tribulation, in those days shall the sun be darkened and the moon shall not give her light and the stars shall fall from heaven, and the powers of the heavens will be shaken." But during the days of trouble, the Lord will protect His bride: Psalm 27:5 "For in the time of trouble He shall hide me in His pavilion; in a secret place of His tabernacle He shall hide me; He shall set me high upon a rock." By looking into a Jewish wedding, we can more clearly see the picture of the union of the bride with the Messiah. Remember just before the big day the marriage license is to be obtained prior to the wedding ceremony. It requires two witnesses who are usually chosen from the wedding party to be part in the signing of the license. Anyone who witnesses the wedding can sign as a witness. The document is signed by two witnesses, and has a standing of a legal binding agreement. Remember the two witnesses in the book of Revelation. "These are God's two witnesses. These are my Two Olive Trees, the two candlesticks standing before the God of the earth." – Revelation 11:4.

The Bible says it is appointed for man to die once and then face judgment. Enoch and Elijah are the ones who never died and will come back to earth. There is a lot of controversy about this subject and I would like to clear it up today. Some say this is Moses and Elijah, Malachi 4:5 says "Behold, I will send you Elijah the prophet before the coming of the great and dreadful day of the Lord." Enoch never died so he must be the one coming back. You see it is appointed for men to die once. One question when is Enoch coming back to die? Moses died and God buried him. Second reason is Enoch was a Gentile, and Elijah was a Jew. These are the two witnesses, one for the Jews and one for the Gentiles. (Romans 11:17-24) You have the Two Olive Trees, the natural branches represent the Jews, and the wild branches represent the Gentiles. Romans 11:24,25 "For if thou wert cut out of the olive tree which is wild by nature, and wert grafted contrary to nature into a good olive tree: how much more shall these, which be the natural branches, be grafted into their own olive tree? For I would not, brethren, that you should be ignorant of this mystery, lest you should be wise in your own conceits; that blindness in part is happened to Israel, until the fullness of the Gentiles be come in." Enoch is the seventh (7th) from Adam – Jude 14 (7+14=21). Enoch was a type of the Rapture of the church. But you say "What about the Mountain of Transfiguration?", where God took Peter James and John high on a mountain at Caesarea Philippi.

Let's look at Mark's gospel where he starts when Jesus was 30 years old. For the first 2 1/2 years Jesus forbids anyone to tell who He was, this is not the case for Matthew, Luke or John. This is like a building up from Jordan to Galilee to Caesarea Philippi and then to Mount Hermon all the time Jesus forbids anyone to tell who He was. Mark 8:26-27 "...and He sent him (blind man) away to his house, saying, 'neither go into town, nor tell it to any in the town...' And Jesus went out and His disciples with Him, to the town of Caesarea Philippi: and along the way He asked His disciples, saying unto them, who do men say that I am?'"

At Caesarea Philippi there is a massive wall of rocks that is well over 100 feet straight up about 500 feet wide. The city of Caesarea Philippi was built on top of this enormous rock. It was enlarged and rededicated by King Philip to honor the Caesar in Rome. Caesar considered himself a god and King Philip was eager to please him. The Greeks and the Roman culture had many gods. Another god that was especially honored here in Caesarea Philippi was the pagan god of Pan. Here you have the true God who came as a man, and a man that is worshipped as a god! And now Jesus asked him "Who do men say that I am?" And they answered Him "Some say John the Baptist, some say Elijah, others say you're a prophet" and Peter answered and said to Him "Thou art the Christ, the Son of the Living God."

Mark 9:2-8 "And after six days Jesus took with him Peter, James and John, and leadeth them up into a high mountain apart by themselves, and He was transfigured (The Shekinah Glory) before them. And His raiment became shiny, exceeding white as snow; so as no fuller on earth can white them. And there appeared unto them Elijah with Moses and they were talking with Jesus. And Peter answered and said unto Jesus, 'Master is it good for us to be here; and let us make three tabernacles, one for you, one for Moses, and one for Elijah'. For he wist not what to say; for they were so afraid. And there was a cloud that overshadowed them; and a voice came out of the cloud, saying, 'This is My beloved Son; hear Him.'" This is a shadow of the Trinity, the Father, the Law and the Prophets. Moses represents the Law and Elijah represents the prophets, Matthew 22:37-40 ..." On these two commandments depend the whole law and the prophets." Matthew 7:12 "In everything, therefore, treat people the same way you want them to treat you, this is the law and the prophets."

Law plus the prophets equals Jesus. Notice after the sixth (6th) day (or 6000 years) Jesus took Peter, James and John (all the church in heaven) and a shadow of us as we are bowing before the Father, Son, and Holy Spirit and the Shekinah Glory in Heaven where we rule and reign with Christ 1000 years = 7000 Years. On the eighth (8th) day a new heaven and a new earth. The number eight (8) means new beginning. Let's look at the maid of honor and the best man, and who would you say it is? We have a best man to the Jew and a maid of honor/best man to the Gentile. John the Baptist: the friend of the bridegroom – John 3:29 and best man to the Jew. Unlike his disciples the Baptist is filled with joy, the joy of a best man at a wedding and Paul who is the best man to the Gentile Bride.

The friend of the bridegroom was to wait outside the bridal chamber for the groom, indicating that the marriage had been consummated in intercourse. So John drew on that word picture: he was a friend of the bridegroom... The "Shoshben" in Hebrew. Now the Shoshben had a unique place at a Jewish wedding. He delivered the invitations and set everything up for the wedding feast. And when all this was done he had one more very special duty. You see, after the ceremony, it was his job to be the liaison between the bride and the bridegroom. It was his task to guard the bedchamber where the bride waited and let no false lover in. He would only open the door when he heard and recognized the bridegroom's voice. When he did, he let the groom in and then went away rejoicing for his task was completed. He did not begrudge the bridegroom and the bride their joy. He knew that his only task had been to bring them together and when that was done, he willingly and gladly faded out of the picture. In Matthew 11:11 Jesus said "I tell you the truth: among those born of women, there has not risen anyone greater than John the Baptist." What a toast!!!

Paul the apostle said to the Gentiles "Through Him and for His Namesake, we received grace and apostleship to call people from among all the Gentiles to the obedience that comes through faith" – Romans 1:5 Paul responsibility was to bring the Gentiles into the righteousness relationship with the God of Israel through the new covenant which Messiah brought. He makes this very clear throughout his letters. His primary audience is Gentile believers. Every time Paul refers to himself as an apostle, he is reminding his audience of his God-given authority to the Gentiles. He was very conscientious of his particular calling. Salvation starts with the Jews and finishes with the Gentiles and God is going back to the Gentiles. After our Big Wedding we shall be called Mr. and Mrs. "THE LORD OUR RIGHTEOUSNESS". Jeremiah 23:6.... And this is his name hereby he (Man) shall be called, "THE LORD OUR RIGHTEOUSNESS". Jeremiah 33:16.... "And this is the name wherewith she (Woman) shall be called, "THE LORD OUR RIGHTEOUSNESS."

We take on God's last name forever and forever "JEHOVAH-TSIDKENU RIGHTEOUSNESS." Israel is the bride of God – Isaiah 54:5. The church is the bride of Christ – Matthew 25:1-46. The sun is even likened to a bridegroom coming out of his chamber – Psalm 19:45. The Bible is our marriage covenant contract known as a Ketubah – John 3:16. The bride must give her consent and say "I DO "- Exodus 24:3 & Romans 10:8-10. The bride and groom are betrothed to each other to court each other – Jeremiah 2:2 & Hosea 2:19-20. The Holy Spirit is our chaperone – John 14:16-17. In Judaism they get married under the Chuppah, and as in most cultures the lady takes on the husband's name – Jeremiah 23:6 Man & Jeremiah 33:16 Woman. Gifts were given to the bride and a cup of the covenant was shared between the bride and groom. Holy Spirit – Acts 2:38 & Cup of Wine Jeremiah 31:31-33. The bridegroom went to his father's house to make ready his wife a new home, and Jesus said he would go to prepare a place for us – John 14:1-3. The bride had a mikvah (water immersion) which is a ritual of cleansing. Immersing in the mikvah is considered spiritual rebirth – Luke 3:16. The bride was consecrated and set apart for a period of time – Mark 13:32-37. This is what I meant when I said the Bible is like a big Jewish wedding.

Back to Daniel chapter 12, as we look how the book of Daniel ended in verse two with the Rapture. Daniel 12:2 says "...and many of them that sleep in the dust of the earth shall awake, some to everlasting life, and some to the shame of everlasting contempt. And God told Daniel to seal up this book to the time of the end. Many shall be buffeted by great trials and persecutions. But the wicked shall continue in their wickedness, and none of them will understand. Only those who are willing to learn or know what it means."

Extra! Extra! Read all about it, "May 4, 2012 Europe plots to create a super president to rule all." Extra! Extra! Read all about it; "September 20, 2012 Berlin Group: EU Needs Army and Super-President." Extra! Extra! Read all about it: May 4, 2012 EU plot to scrap Britain senior Eurocrats are secretly plotting to create a Super- Powerful EU president to realize their dream of abolishing Britain, we can reveal. Extra! Extra! Read all about it: July 7, 2009 Pope Urges Forming New World Economy Order to work for the "Common Good", on Tuesday called for a radical rethinking of the global economy, criticizing a growing divide between rich and poor and urging the establishment of a "true world political authority" to oversee the economy and work for the "common good." Extra! Extra! Read all about it: Daily Mail.com May 4, 2012 Britain under threat from plot to create super-powerful EU president "…that will mean the end to nation states".

The world right now is looking for someone to fix the problems of the world. The Bible, written over 2000 years ago, foretold that there was coming a World Leader call the Antichrist. The Bible said that he (the Antichrist) will come out of the 10 horns which are 10 kings. Daniel chapter 7:20,25 "…and of the 10 horns that were in his head, and of the other which came up, and before whom three fell; even of that which had eyes, and a mouth that speaks very great things, whose look is more stout than his followers. vs 25. And he (Antichrist)shall speak great words against the Most High and shall wear out the saints of the Most High, and think to change times (Jewish calendar into Pagan calendar) and laws (God's law into Pagan law); and they shall be given unto his hands until a time and times and the dividing of time (3 ½ years).

Do I think the Antichrist is alive today? Yes I do! Do I know who he is? No I don't! I have my guesses! Make no mistake about it for the first 3 1/2 years of the tribulation, he will be sweet as mom's apple pie. His charm and charisma will be unmatched and the world will love Him. But the last 3 ½ years he will be the worst you've ever seen, and make

Hitler look like a baby.

Extra! Extra! Read all about it: Los Angeles Times Wednesday May 12, 1999 The Devil in Disguise? As the new millennium nears believers are steadfast: the Antichrist is at large, and the coming battle between good and evil will unmask him. Throughout history and even up until today people have said and wondered, who is this Man? I guess after the tribulation when all the saints come back with Christ to fight him (Antichrist) at Armageddon maybe then we'll know.

HAROLD BALL

Chapter 7

REVELATION:

Like You've Never Seen It Before

The Book of Revelation: God's signature and fingerprints The Number Seven

My purpose in this book is not to put down anyone's religion, but to show God's truths proving that He is the King of Kings and Lord of lords.

The unique feature in the book of Revelation is the number seven. 1. Seven churches, Seven cities, Seven letters, Seven spirits, Seven golden lampstands, Seven stars, Seven seals, Seven horns, Seven eyes, Seven angels, Seven trumpets, Seven thunders, Seven thousand, Seven heads, Seven grounds, Seven plagues, Seven bowls, Seven mountains, Seven kings, Seven hills, Seven visions, Seven vials and these words occur seven times in the book of Revelation:

1. God's prophets 10:7; 11:18; 16:6; 18:20; 18:24; 22:6; 22:9 / 2. Earthquake 6:12; 8:5; 11:13 (2); 11:19; 16:18 (2) / 3. Blessed   1:3; 14:13; 16:15; 19:9; 20:6; 22:7; 22:14 / 4. Christ's sword 1:16; 2:12; 2:16; 13:10; 19:15; 19:21 (2) / 5. Candlestick 1:12; 1:13; 1:20 (2); 2:1; 2:5; 11:4 / 6. Christ's blood   1:5; 5:6; 5:9; 5:12; 7:14; 12:11; 13:8 / 7. Book of life   3:5; 13:8; 17:8; 20:12; 20:15; 21:27; 22:19 / 8. Prophecy   1:3; 11:6; 19:10; 22:7; 22:10; 22:18; 22:19 / 9. Day, Night   4:8; 7:15; 8:12; 12:10; 14:11; 20:10; 21:25

10. "He that hath an ear, let him hear what the Spirit saith unto the churches" Revelation 2:7; 2:11; 2:17; 2:29; 3:6; 3:13; 3:22.

The book of Revelation has 22 chapters and the Hebrew alphabet has 22 letters. The 21st letter of the Hebrew alphabet is called – SHIN. The letter SHIN, being equivalent to the number 300 in the Hebrew alphabet, and represents defined power as it is the initial letter of two of the names of God. Shaddai, one of the names of God, begins with the letter SHIN. The word Shaddai is usually translated into English as "Almighty". In English it looks like a big W. and most of all the Jewish homes, hotels and synagogues have this on the front door meaning "God is our protector" "when passing through the door, one must touch and kiss the words, Shaddai, and recite the following prayer: "May God protect my going out and my going in from now on and for evermore." In Hebrew this is called the Mezuzot.

Here are some secrets of the Hebrew letters, the seventh letter of the Hebrew alphabet is called "Zayin" which means Sword. Since Zayin represents a crowned Man, we would expect it to reveal another truth about Jesus as King of the Jews, since Zayin's sword represents our protector, as Jesus is the Lion of the tribe of Judah, and since Zayin also represents nourishment life, Jesus is here depicted as the shepherd who feeds His sheep. The sword mentioned in Hebrews 4:12 is (machaira) a short sword that was sharpened on both edges of the blade. The two edges represent the two main parts of the Scriptures (the Old Testament and the New Testament). EL Shaddai means God Almighty and it is also here in Israel where God wrote His name. 1 Kings 11:36 "And unto his son will I give one tribe, that David My servant may have a light, a way before me in Jerusalem, the city in which I have chosen Me to put My name there."

If you look through a satellite map down on Jerusalem you will see God's name SHIN. The 21st letter of the Hebrew alphabet is SHIN (777). In Jerusalem there are three valleys 1. Hinnom Valley 2. Tyropoeon Valley 3. Kidron Valley and it is shaped like the letter SHIN. In the Old Testament El Shaddai occurs seven (7) times. Just as Jews are taught to reverence God Himself, they are also taught to revere His name, especially when speaking or writing one of the seven (7) names of God. 1. El, 2. Elohim, 3. YHVH, 4.Adonai, 5. Ehyeh asher ehyeh, 6. Shaddai, 7. Tzava'ot.

The Jewish scribes must wipe the pen and wash their entire bodies before writing the most holy name of God, every time they wrote it. The name Jehovah is in your Bible seven (7) times 1. Exodus 6:3, 2.Psalms 83:18, Isaiah 12:2, Isaiah 26:4, Genesis 22:14, Exodus 17:15, Judges 6:24. Jehovah has seven (7) letters. **In the Hebrew alphabet YHVH means "behold the hands" "behold the nails".** Passover is in the King James Bible 77 times and is on the 14th day (7+7=14). Amazing. The blood Moon on Passover that happened on April 15, 2014 was actually on Nisan 14 of the Jewish calendar and lasted 77 minutes.

Jesus' genealogy according to Luke starting with God 1. God, 2. Adam 3. Seth 4. Enosh 5. Kenan ...to 77 Jesus is 77. Church is in the King James Bible 77 times, Amen is in the KJ Bible 77 times, Verily I say unto thee.. In the KJ Bible 77 times, Watchmen in the KJ Bible 14 times, Twenty One in the KJ Bible only ONE Time, First and The Last in the KJ Bible Seven (7) times: 1. Isaiah 41.4 / 2. Isaiah 44:6 / 3. Isaiah 48:12 / 4. Revelation 1:11 / 5. Revelation 1:17 / 6.

Revelation 2:8 / 7. Revelation 22:13. Prophecy is in the KJ Bible 21 times. Scriptures in the KJ Bible 21 times. There are 31,102 versus in the KJ Bible add up to "7" (3+1+1+0+2=7). Before I go on and on and on about God's signature let's get started on the book of Revelation.

The Revelation is the only book in the Bible where God gives a special blessing to the reader and the hearer. Revelation 1:3 "Blessed is he that reads and hears the words of this prophecy..." I used to wonder why God only picked seven churches, there were many other churches at that time; it would seem to be more historically significant than the seven that Jesus addressed: the churches at Jerusalem, Galatia, Corinth, Antioch, Rome, Lystra, Derbe, Colossae, Troas, Hierapolis, to name a few. Why did Jesus select just these seven? The seven churches of Revelation are 1. Ephesus the Loveless Church, forsook its 1ST love 2. Smyrna the Persecuted Church, Tribulation Saints, 3. Pergamos the Compromising Church, Needed to Repent, 4. Thyatira the Corrupt Church, had a False Prophetess, 5. Sardis the Dead Church, They Fell Asleep, 6. Philadelphia, the Faithful Church, endured patiently, 7. Laodicea, the Lukewarm Church, love God, love Sin.

I believe that the seven churches are seven types of people in the body of Christ. I believe you can find one of these persons in the body of Christ all over the world. When you read the seven churches you put yourself in one of these churches. The Angel that God is speaking to are the Shepherds and Pastors of these churches. Every church in the world has one of these types of people in the church. God is speaking to the body of Christ. Philadelphia is the only church that is obeying God. God signs His approval with the number SEVEN on these churches. 1.

Seven Churches, 2. Seven Cities, 3.Seven Letters, (777), and all seven churches are written in order that you can look down from space and you can see the number Seven (7) written on the world. (PICTURE 5) There is one church here that I was confused on until God opened up my understanding and it is the church of Smyrna. Revelation 2:8 " and unto the Angel of the church in Smyrna write; these things saith the First and the Last, which was dead, and is alive; 9. I know thy works, and tribulation, and poverty, but thou are rich and I know the blasphemy of them which say they are Jews, and are not, but they are from the synagogue of Satan. 10. Fear none of those things which thou shalt suffer: behold, the devil shall cast some of you in prison, that ye may be tried; and you shall have tribulation 10 days; but be faithful unto death; and I will give you the crown of life".

The church at Smyrna is the Tribulation Saints (church) that will go through the seven year tribulation. These are the five churches (Ephesus, Pergamum, Thyatira, Sardis and Laodicea) that Jesus removed His candlestick from. These are backsliders, lukewarm, carnal Christians that realize they didn't make the rapture and now must pay with their life. Everybody that does not give their allegiance to the Antichrist will be tortured and killed. If you manage to escape for seven years without him finding you, without taking the mark of the beast, you will be going to the millennial reign. But for all those that will lose their life for Jesus will gain their life. 1. Fear none of those things which thou shalt suffer; torture, chased, beat up. 2. The Antichrist shall cast some of you in prison; FEMA camps, concentration camps. 3. That ye may be tried; stand before a judge, stand in front of a jury, deny Jesus or die. 4. You should have Tribulation 10 days; this is the

Seven Year Tribulation Period.

John who wrote the book of Revelation would know exactly what this meant because he was a Jew. Rosh Hashanah is the rapture of the church, and Yom Kippur - the Day of Atonement is when Jesus physically comes back to earth. Rosh Hashanah is on Tishri 1 and Yom Kippur is on Tishri 10, exactly 10 days apart. John was speaking in Jewish terms for God's Feast Days. Rosh Hashanah is seven "years" from Yom Kippur. 10 Days = 7 Years. There is a difference between martyrs and the Tribulation Saints. A martyr is someone that dies for Christ *before* the Tribulation Period. A Tribulation Saint is someone who dies for Christ *during* the Tribulation. Revelation 7:13-14 "...and one of the elders answered, saying unto me, what are these which are arrayed in white robes? 14. And I said unto him, Sir, thou knowest. And he said unto me, these are they which came out of the great tribulation, and have washed their robes, and made them white in the blood of the Lamb.

Well you might be asking "who are these in Revelation 6:9? "And we know he had opened the fifth seal, I saw under the altar the souls of them that were slain for the word of God, and for the testimony (the word of God) which they held; 10. And they cried with a loud voice, saying, how long, O Lord, holy and true, dost thou not (when are you going to) Judge and avenge our blood on them that will only be on earth? 11. In white robes were given unto every one of them; and it was said unto them (Jesus said to them), that they should rest yet for a little season (a little more time), until their fellow servants (martyr's) also and their brethren, that should be killed as they were, should be fulfilled (a lot of martyrs are being killed today). This is the Fifth Seal and God has not sent his Judgment to the world. The Judgment is the Tribulation Period. If the Tribulation were started already, they would not be asking God when He is going to send the judgment and avenge us. God will be doing it already but God said wait a little while longer. They would not need to ask God this question if the Tribulation had started.

Some people think that the tribulation period started in Revelation 4, and no seals were open. Actually the Tribulation starts at the Sixth Seal, and First Seal, Second Seal, Third Seal, Fourth Seal, and Fifth Seal are all open. We are waiting on the Sixth Seal to open and lo there was a great earthquake; and the sun became black as sackcloth of hair, and the moon became as blood: Blood Moon and a Solar Eclipse. And Stephen was the first martyr and they keep going to the Day of Judgment but until then they are asking God how long before you judge them on the earth killing us? And once the Tribulation starts, God would avenge their blood. Today all of the martyrs are asking God to avenge them and to send judgement.

Here are two keys to understanding the book of Revelation, one -- the book of Revelation is divided (Rev. 1:19) into; 1) 'the things which thou hast seen" events of chapter 1, 2.) "The things which are" - the seven churches that exist at the time and to which John wrote in chapters 2 & 3, (i.e....) there are more than seven churches). Believers in every church can learn from what was written to each of the seven churches that existed in John's day.) Examine your own life, and where are you with God?, 3.) "The things which shall be here after" events from chapter 4 until the end of chapter 22. (Rev 4:1). Secondly, the book of Revelation is in order, but is not in chronological order. The Hebrew biblical way of thinking, writing is cyclical with additional information presented in each retelling of the story. For example: was Jesus crucified one time or four times? He was crucified once, of course, but the story is told, in total, from four perspectives: Matthew, Mark, then Luke, then John tells us about the life of Jesus in their Gospels, each looping back to commence at a previous point in the story, and each adding pieces to the puzzle or confirming (by two or three witnesses) the events that were reported to have occurred. Genesis chapter 1 describes creation. Genesis chapter 2 loops back (not all the way to the beginning though) and provides more detail about some of the events. Likewise, from chapter 4 to chapter 22 the book of Revelation loops back to a previous point in time (not all the way to the beginning nor to the beginning of the previous loop) and begins to re-tell a story with more details provided on each retelling. The seven seals tell a long story (from just after Jesus time on earth), and ends at Armageddon. (Rev 6). The seventh trumpet tell the shorter story (from World War I), and ends at the battle of Armageddon. (Rev 11). The seven veils tell the really short story (beginning at prior to the battle of Armageddon, and ends at the end of the battle of Armageddon. (Rev 16). This way you can get a better understanding and a much clearer picture of the book of Revelation.

Let's start with the seven seals in Revelation 6:1, "and I saw when the Lamb open one of the seals, and I heard, as it were the noise of thunder, one of the four beasts saying, come and see. And I saw and behold a WHITE HORSE and he that sat on him had a bow; and a crown was given unto him: and he went forth conquering, and to conquer." The first thing I notice is that God opens up the seals. Many people think that this is a picture of the Antichrist but when it comes to the next three seals they have no idea who they are. But actually the Bible calls these horses spirits Zachariah 1:8-11 says "and I saw by night, and behold a man riding on a red horse, and he stood among the myrtle trees that were in the bottom, and behind him were Red horses, a speckled horse, and white horse. Then said I, O my lord, what are these? And the angel that talked with me said unto me, I will show you what they are, And the man that stood among the myrtle trees answered and said, these are they whom the Lord has sent to walk, to and fro (back and forth) through the earth. And they (spirits) answered the angel of the Lord that stood among the myrtle trees, and said, we (the spirits) have walked to and fro (back and forth) through the earth, and, behold, all the earth sitteth still, and is at rest." Zachariah 6:1-7 says "and I turned, and lifted up mine eyes, and looked, and, behold, there came four chariots out a between two mountains; and the mountains were mountains of brass. In the first chariot were red horses; and in the second chariots were black horses; and in the third chariot white horses; and in the fourth chariot bay horses (pale or green). Then I answered and said unto the angel that talked with me, what are these, my lord? And the angel answered and said unto me, THESE ARE THE FOUR SPIRITS OF THE HEAVENS, which go forth (back and forth) from standing before the Lord of all the earth. The black horses which are therein go forth unto the North Country; and the white horses go forth after them; and the (pale or green) go forth toward the South country. And the bay (Red) went forth, and sought to go that they might walk to and fro (back and forth) through the earth: and he said, Get you hence ("Go. Begin your patrol." So they left at once), walk to and fro (back and forth) through the earth. So they walked to and fro through the earth. Then the Lord summoned me and said, "Those who went north have executed my judgment, and quieted my anger there."

The Four Horses of the Apocalypse are spirits of the Lord to do His bidding and execute His judgments. Let's take a look at spirits -- when I was in school we had what was called our team spirit. We would buy banners and waive flags and shout our team logo. The spirit was strong and moved the school crowds. Today we have for strong spirits that move nations. So let's look at the WHITE HORSE in Revelation 6:2. I believe that one of those spirits is the spirit of Catholicism. This is a very, very strong spirit, millions have died behind this spirit and this spirit is 1 billion+ strong. The rider on the white horse is the spirit of Catholicism. 1. And he that sat on him had a bow = his own doctrine, 2. A crown was given to him = the Pope and the Papal Tiara's symbolic Power. Over the course of the church's history, the papal crown has developed a long and interesting history of its own. Benedict XVI no longer wears it even though it was recently presented to him by a group of Roman Catholics and Eastern Orthodox Christians. - Vatican insider. 3. He went forth conquering and to conquer; = Conquer the World for Christ! "Give me an army saying the rosary and I will conquer the world." - Pope Pius IX. The spirit of a nation always waves his flag, so what color is the flag of Catholicism? White. The White horse is a clear picture of someone that wants to imitate Christ and looks like a lamb but speaks like a dragon. Would that be the political leader (antichrist) or the religious leader (false prophet)? Do you know the Pope's favorite color? White. His clothing is white, his Pope Mobile is white, his van is white, his Land Rover is white, his bus is white, his yacht is white, his train is white, his bicycle is white, his statue is white, his helicopter is white, his airplane is white, his umbrella is white, what color would his horse be? You see long before you can remember the most important ceremony making an election of a new Pope was the procession which accompanied him from the Vatican to S. Giovanni in Laterano, the ancient site of the Papal. The procession was called possession as the Pope by crossing the whole city took possession of Rome. The Pope reached S. Giovanni in Laterano writing a white horse. Pope Martin V is seen on a white horse lead by his Emperor. The previous century had seen its climax of the Papal power. Towards the close (AD – 1294) Boniface VIII became Pope. His inauguration was the most magnificent that had ever been known. He rode through Rome on a white horse, a Crown on his head, his bridle held by two kings, the nobility of Rome in his train. So the rider on the White Horse is Catholicism.

So let's look at the RED HORSE in Revelation 6:4 "and there went out another horse that was Red, and power was given to him that set thereon to take peace from the earth, and that they should kill one another; and there was given unto him a great sword. This is the spirit of Communism and their flag is Red. This is a very strong spirit and millions have died by the spirit of Communism.

Which countries possess Communism? 1. Red Russia, 2. Red China, 3. Red Army. 1. And they came to take peace from the earth = they just formed what is called "THE BRICK NATION", they both had a flag with the sickle and the hammer. 2. And that they should kill one another; they're always fighting against their brethren, Ukraine, Georgia, Kyrgyzstan, Japan, North Korea, and South Korea.

3. And there was given unto them a great sword; The Sword of Victory = three huge tall monuments were built in three locations – Ural Mountains in central Russia to Berlin, Germany. All three monuments were constructed by one item. It was a huge metal sword of victory – Russia. China is always known for its sword, the statue of Guan Gong in Yuncheng City – China he is one of the famous Chinese generals during the late Eastern Han Dynasty and three kingdoms era of China (206 BC – 220 AD). He was always caring one Guan Dao Sword. They call themselves Red China and Red Russia, the Communist Nations. China's population is 1.4 billion people compared to the United States population at 316 million.

So let's look at the BLACK HORSE discussed in Revelation 6:5 "and when he (Lamb) had opened the seal, I heard the third say, come and see. And I beheld, and lo a BLACK HORSE; and he sat on him had a pair of balances in his hand. 6. And I heard a voice in the midst of the four beasts say, a measure of wheat for a penny, and three measures of barley for a penny; and see thou hurt not the oil and the wine. This is the Black Horse of Capitalism, and this is a very strong spirit. And millions of people have died over capitalism because it is the love of money. City of London, Friday, October 10, 2008 protesters hurling signs and banners and one sign reads from newspaper; SOCIALIST WORKER "Capitalism isn't working." And another sign read "No Bailout No Capitalism." Guess what color flag that you would hold up if you was a capitalist? You guessed it!!! A "Black Flag." Is called the black flag of capitalism. We live in a capitalist society where the one who makes the rules makes the money. Do you know the difference between capitalism and socialism? Let's say we're in school, and the teacher in the classroom says "I'm going to take everybody's grades A, B, C, D and average them out. That way we all can get the same grade" so if you study and got an A and somebody else did not study and got a D, we all would get a B- or C+. Would that be okay with you? This is what is meant by socialists. The problem with that is the students that stayed up all night long and studied would say "why should I study so hard and stay up all night long, when all the other students are not studying and getting a better grade?" So the students will stop studying and be like the students getting a D, so they all start failing and this is called socialism. Capitalism is when you make an "A" and you keep your "A" and you don't share it with anyone. If you get an "F" for not studying you get what you deserve. The problem with this is you create greed. You thought of the company, and you created it, and therefore you take all the money or set your own salary. And you really don't care about anyone else and this is called capitalism. Let's take a closer look at the Scriptures; 1. And he that sat on him had a pair of balances in his hand = look on the front of your dollar bill on the great seal and you will see a pair of balances. 2. A measure of wheat for a penny and three measures of barley for a penny = these are stock market terms. In the stock market everything goes up and down by the pennies. Wheat and barley are traded by the pennies. A long time ago when you bought items and goods you set them on a scale. At that scale price you would know what to pay for wheat, flour, sugar, candy. etc. 3. See that you do not hurt the oil and the wine; (maybe his believers) I believe it has a spiritual meaning but God hasn't open my eyes to this one yet!!!.

So let's look at the PALE HORSE Revelation 6:7 and when he had opened the forth seal, I heard the voice of the fourth beast say, come and see. 8. And I looked, and behold a PALE HORSE; and his name that sat on him was Death, and Hell followed with him. And power was given unto him over the fourth part of the earth, to kill with a sword, and with hunger, and with death, and with the beast of the earth. First of all this pale horse is not really pale at all!!! This Pale means Green. If you look in the concordance for the number 5515 you will see that it means Green.

This is the Spirit of Islam and they are 1.8 Billion people strong. This spirit has killed millions of people and is called the GREEN HORSE of Islam. They fly their flags high, the Green flag of Islam. So let's look at the GREEN HORSE Revelation 6:8 says 1. "And his name that set on him was Death, and Hell followed him;" "Death to America" "Death to Israel" "USA Go to Hell" "Death to the Jews and to America" look for yourselves on YouTube: HAMAS: In Their Own Voices – Death to Jews / America. 2. And power was given unto him over the fourth part of the earth; Muslims in the world today represent one-quarter percent of the world's population. Google: Muslims as a Share of world population, 1990-2030. One-quarter percent of 7.2 billion people = 1.8 billion Muslims. Today the Muslims have a fourth part of the Earth. 3. And to kill with sword; they love to cut off head, hands, they love to bring death by the sword. 4. And with hunger; what do they produce? Besides oil? 5. And with the beast of the earth; The Return of The Mahdi: Throughout the Islamic world today there is a call for the restoration of the Islamic Caliphate.

The Caliph in Islam may be viewed somewhat as a Pope of the Muslims. The Caliph is viewed as a vice-reagent for Allah on the earth. It is important to understand that when Muslims call for the restoration of the Caliphate, it is ultimately the Mahdi that they are calling for. For the Mahdi is the awaited final Caliph of Islam. As such, Muslims everywhere will be obligated to follow the Mahdi. "One Man To Unite Them All." Google: "Was Muhammad A True Prophet? – Miracles of Mohammed and Christ www.thespiritofislam.com.

THE FIFTH SEAL: What is the difference between a martyr and a tribulation saint? Revelation 6:9 "and when he had opened the FIFTH (5th) SEAL, I saw under the altar the souls of them that were slain for the word of God, and for the testimony (faithful to Jesus) which they (martyrs) held. 10. "And they (martyrs) cried with a loud voice, saying, how long, O Lord, holy and true, dost thou not judge and avenge our blood on them that will be on the earth? (How long will it be before you judge the people of the earth for what they've done to us?) When will you avenge the blood against those living on the earth?). 11. And white robes were given to every one of them (martyrs); and it was said unto them, that they should rest yet for a little season, until their fellow-servants also and their brethren (Messianic Jew/Christian Gentile), that should he killed as they were, should be fulfilled."

There is a difference between martyrs and tribulation saints, (Revelation 7:13-14 speaks about the tribulation saints which is during the opening of the Sixth Seal). These are martyrs and not tribulation saints, notice that they are asking God to avenge them for being killed. Notice God's response "wait a little bit longer until the martyrs in China, martyrs in Syria, martyrs in North Korea, martyrs in Africa, martyrs all over the world, then and only then will I send my judgment to the world. If the tribulation had started already they would not be asking God this question. If God would have started his judgment the tribulation, Day of the Lord, they need not ask "how long O Lord will use in your judgment". The fifth seal is open and the martyrs are crying out today. So let's look at Revelation 6:12 "and I beheld when he had opened the SIXTH (6th) SEAL, and, lo, there were as a great earthquake; and the sun became black as sackcloth of hair, and the moon became as blood." The Time of Jacob's Trouble: Jeremiah 30:7 which says, "Alas! For that Day is Great, so that none is like it: it is even the time of Jacob's Trouble; but he shall be saved out of it." Jeremiah 30:7 says, "That day is great, so that none is like it." The only time period that fits this description is the period of the Tribulation. This time is unparalleled in history. The opening of the 6th Seal triggers the Rapture and the Day of the Lord, the time at which God will pour out his wrath on the unbelieving world. With the cataclysmic global earthquake and a Solar Eclipse and a Blood Moon proves these events are of divine origin. This shaking of Heaven and Earth is the time that God rises to personally intervene and judge the centuries of sin and evil of His unbelieving, unrepentant world. It is also a wake-up call to Israel to return to the worship of the God of their fathers, the God of Abraham Isaac and Jacob. 13. "And the stars of heaven fail unto the earth, even as a fig tree cast her untimely figs, when she is shaking of a mighty wind." 14. "And the heaven departed as a scroll when it is rolled together; and every mountain and island were moved out of their places." Zachariah 14:12 "and this shall be the plague wherewith the Lord will smite all the people that have fought against Jerusalem; their flesh shall consume a way while they stand upon their feet, and her eyes shall consume a way in their holes, and their tongue shall consume away in their mouth."

This sounds like a Neutron bomb twice the lethal range of a 10 kt nuclear device. Kills all living things with a massive wave of radiation. Leaves most buildings / armaments intact. The world is full of nuclear bombs and is not how it would happen but when will it happen. God says in Ezekiel 38:4 "and I (God) will turn the back, and put hooks into thy jaws, and I (God) will bring the forth, and all thy armies, horses and horsemen, all of them clothed with all sorts of armor, even a great company with bucklers and Shields, all of them handling swords." God said he would bring these armies to Israel and he will destroy them there, and Israel will live off of the fuel of that war for Seven years. (Ezekiel 39:9 …. And they shall burn them with fire Seven (7) years"). And it would take Israel Seven (7) months to bury the dead and that place will be called Hamon-gog (Ezekiel 39:12-15). You might ask, "Why would God do this?" For his namesake! "For 1) the kings of the earth, 2) the great men, 3) the rich man, 4) the chief captains, 5) the mighty men, 6) every bondsman, and 7) every freeman, hid themselves in the dance and in the rocks of the mountains." The rich are rushing to build end-of-the-world bunkers, Ron Laytner and Martin Ferko underground bunkers are believed to be everywhere; below the streets in Washington and New York Red Square in Moscow. Even Northern Ireland, population 1.7 million has a 223 person nuclear bunker at Ballymena in County Antrim. And the much threatened Wiki-leaks server is located in an old nuclear bunker and Sweden.

Extra! Extra! Read all about it: THE RICHEST March 22, 2014 Billionaire Bunkers: How The Rich Prepare For Doomsday. Notice 1. The kings, 2. Great men, 3. Rich men, 4. Chief Captains, 5.mighty men, 6. Bondsman, 7. Freeman - all Seven (7) different types. 16. "And said to the mountains and rocks, fall on us, and hide us from the face of Him that sitteth on the throne, and from the wrath of the Lamb: 17. For the great day of His wrath is come; and who shall be able to stand? On The Day of The Lord the Bible says that's a day of darkness not light – Amos 5:18 "Woe unto you that desire the day of the Lord! To what end is it for you? The day of the Lord is darkness, and not light.

So let's go on to Revelation Chapter 7 and notice the angel with the sixth seal still in his hand. 7:1 "and after these things I saw the four angels standing on the four corners of the earth, holding the four winds of the earth, that the wind should not blow on the earth, nor the sea, nor any tree(No wind blowing). 2. And I saw another angel ascending from the East, having the Seal (sixth seal) of the living God: and He cried with a loud voice to the four angels, to it was given to hurt earth and the sea, 3. Saying, hurt not the earth, neither the sea, nor the trees, till we have sealed the servants of our God in their foreheads." After the rapture of the church an angel will tell the four other angels to wait till he seals the 144,000 Jews in their foreheads before they start destroying the earth. During this seven years there are going to be a lot of plagues and death also, like God put Noah on the ark and left the door open for seven days, because of His love and mercy, will again show His love and mercy during the seven-year tribulation. Even then God is going to allow all those people that are from those five churches in revelation and whoever else that repents and turns to Him during the tribulation will be saved. But this time you're going to have to pay with your life. "And they are called tribulation saints, and for this you will get the crown of life."

Like Noah, God waited seven days to close the door, God will wait seven years and close the door. That is why Yom Kippur "Neilah" means the closing of the gates. Revelation 7:11 "and all the angels stood around about the throne, about the elders and the four beasts, and fell before the throne on their faces, and worshipped God. 12. Saying, Amen: Blessing, and glory, and wisdom, and Thanksgiving, and honor, and power, and might, be unto our God forever and ever Amen."

Notice the seven words we will say to our God: 1. Blessing, 2. Glory, 3. Wisdom, 4. Thanksgiving, 5. Honor, 6. Power, 7. Might. We will all be there on Yom Kippur. Rev. 7:13. "And one of the elders answer, saying unto me, what are these which are arrayed in white robes? And whence came they? (Where do they come from?)." Let's see if you'll get this picture: the rapture of the church happens and we go to Heaven. We have been in heaven for a while, so we look over and see more people in white robes which were not taken up in the rapture, but came up later. Some may ask "who are these?"" Where do they come from?" Revelation 7:14 "and I said unto him, Sir, thou knowest ("no sir" "please tell me"). And he said to me, these are they which came out of the Great Tribulation, and have washed their robes, and made them white in the blood of the Lamb."

These are the ones that realize that Christ is the Messiah and paid the ultimate price for that belief. These are the tribulation saints, that said "I did not believe then but I believe now, and now I would die for that belief that Jesus is the Messiah." These are the ones that say "I'm sorry Lord for doubting You, they can kill me, but I will not doubt You again." The first shall be last and the last shall be first,

Blessed be the Name of the Lord, Amen. Revelation 7:17 "for the Lamb which is in the midst of the throne shall feed them, and shall lead them into living fountains of water: and God shall wipe away all the tears from their eyes.

So let's to the SEVENTH SEAL: Revelation chapter 8. Now remember when I told you from chapter 4 to chapter 22 the Book of Revelation loops back to a previous point in time (not all the way to the beginning nor to the beginning of the previous loop) and begins to re-tell a story with more details provided on each retelling. This is a prime example when we read Revelation chapter 8. Revelation 8:1 "and when he had opened the seventh seal, there was silence in heaven about the space of half an hour. 2. And I saw the seven angels which did bow before God; and to them were given Seven Trumpets." Now this first trumpet takes us back to 1914 with more detail. Revelation 8:6 "and the seventh angel which had the Seven Trumpet prepared themselves to sound. Revelation 7: The FIRST ANGEL SOUNDED, and there followed Hail, and fire mingled with blood, and they were cast upon the earth: and the third part (1/3) (only in that nation) of trees was burned up, and (1/3 of that nation) all green grass was burned up." I believe that this trumpet was World War I from July 28, 1914 to November 11, 1918 which killed 8.2 million people: 1) World War I prepared the land for the return of the Jews with the Balfour declaration. 2) The third part of the trees was burnt up in all green grass was burnt up; fire itself remained a part of warfare. During World War I, Leuven, in Belgium was "looted and burned in medieval fashion", when German soldiers set fires to many of the towns, destroying the libraries and other critical buildings, and causing outrage around the world.

The flamethrower is a potent weapon with great psychological impact upon unprepared soldiers, inflicting a particularly horrific death. This has led to some calls for the weapon to be banned. The Jellied gasoline products had been in use since the days of trench warfare in World War I as a backpacked flamethrower also called German Flamethrower Pioneers of World War I. World War I was one of the bloodiest events; this demolished almost 1/3 of European population. Revelation 8:8 "and The SECOND ANGEL SOUNDED, and as it were a great mountain burning with fire and cast into the sea: and the third part (1/3) (only in that waters) of the sea became blood; 9. And they third part (1/3) (only in that ocean) of the creatures which were in the sea, and had life, died; and the third part (1/3) (only in that war) of the ships were destroyed." I believe this trumpet is World War II September 1, 1939 to September 2, 1945: 1) World War II which brought the Jews back into their land. Birth Pains (sorrows) that gave birth to the nation of Israel. 2) 1/3 Sea, Fish, ship; there were 105,127 warships participating in World War II, 36,387 , (1/3) of the ships were destroyed by the end of the war. A big problem now is that these sunken ships are still leaking hazardous fluids into the ocean. This causes pollution and massive fires. As early as 1942, 287 ships were sunk in the United States and in Canadian waters, without our awareness, 548,884,740,00 liters of oil spilled within 80 km of the coast. To put this in perspective the Exxon Valdez, a supertanker spilled 41,639,532,00 liters of oil. That's an estimated 227,124,72 liters of oil spilled per day every day for six months, creating pollution and harmful to sea life. In World War II approximately 70 million people were killed. Revelation 8:10 "and The THIRD ANGEL SOUNDED, and their fell a Great Star from heaven, burning as it were a lamp, and it fell on the third part of the rivers, and upon the fountains of waters (drinking water); 11. And the name of the star is called wormwood: and the third part of the waters became wormwood; and many men died of the waters because they were made bitter." I believe this to be the Chernobyl disaster on April 26, 1986: Wormwood means Chernobyl in Ukrainian and you can check this by going to "English-Ukrainian dictionary (Express) and/or look in the Ukrainian New Testament Bible.

The Chernobyl disaster released radioactive material with widespread health and environmental effects pushing it to a major accident to "LEVEL 7". A Level 7 is the highest level of any accident in the world. It was the world's worst nuclear disaster and a safety test at the Chernobyl nuclear power plant in northern Ukraine went badly wrong, and the resulting explosion sent an estimated nine times of radioactive material into the air - that's the equivalent of 90 Hiroshima atomic bombings. Nearly 1 million people died between 1986 and 2004, billions of people worldwide were exposed to radioactive contamination from the disaster.

Most people do not know that the Ukraine carried out one of the worse pogroms against Jews in history in the early years of the country's founding. From 1918 to 1921, the new "Ukrainian people's Republic" murdered around 100,000 Jews. About 50,000 fled the Ukraine to Crimea because their lives were at stake. The German "Einsatzgruppen" (task force) killed approximately One MILLION Jews on Ukrainian soil between September 1939 and June 1941. Hennadiy Yosypovych Udovenko is a Ukrainian politician and diplomat. He has served as minister for foreign affairs of Ukraine, has been the 52nd president of the United Nations Gen. Assembly (1997 – 1998) and a member of the Verkhovna Rada (Parliament) of Ukraine (1998 – 2007). Mr. Hennadiy Udovenko said this at the fifty-second session "It is a great honor and privilege for me to be elected president of the Gen. Assembly of the United Nations. I am very grateful for the support of my candidature by the member states and in particular by members of the regional group of Eastern European countries. ………The current environmental problems also demand our increased attention. The sustainability of the entire ecosystem is put into question by irresponsible exploitation of nature and mismanagement meant the sad illustration of the Chernobyl catastrophe. It happened on the territory of my country, where, to quote the Revelation of St. John the Divine, "there fell a great star from heaven… Upon the third part of the river" although it occurred more than a decade ago, the Chernobyl star of Wormwood still hovers like a Damoclean sword over the world as a bitter reminder for all of us."

Extra! Extra! Read all about it" Time Magazine May 12, 1986 Meltdown Chernobyl Reactor. After the explosion it rained for four days and Cesium 137 rained down into the water. Everything it touched became radioactive. Many people were drinking the contaminated water. One hundred and twenty-five thousand (125,000) people died, with 2 million people infected. I encourage you to look at some of the pictures, they will blow your mind. Romans 12:19 "Dearly beloved, avenge not yourselves, but rather give place unto wrath: for it is written, Vengeance is mine; I will repay, saith the Lord". No one is out of the reach of God. Revelation 8:12 "And the FOURTH ANGEL SOUNDED, and the third part (1/3) of the sun was smitten only of that nation, and the third part (1/3) of the moon only of that nation, and the third part (1/3) of the stars only of that nation; so as the third part (1/3) of them was darkened only of that nation, and the day shone not for a third part (1/3) of it only of that nation, and the night likewise. I believe this is the Kuwaiti Gulf War fires: 1) the Sky was mostly affected in that country the (1/3) Sun, Moon, Stars, Day, Night. NASA Peter Pilewskie, Francisco P. J. Valero, Wnrran Gnra says "Among the more horrific events that occurred during the Gulf War of 1991 was the igniting of the oil fields of Kuwait by invading Iraqi forces. 500 oil wells burned continuously, filling the surrounding skies with blackened smoke which blocked out the sun and turned day into night. The dense smoke clouds from the Kuwaiti oil fires created a barrier preventing solar energy reaching the surface of the earth as well as preventing heat from escaping to space."

Fires burned for ten months and a response to that comprised approximately 11,450 workers from 38 countries used both familiar as well as never before tested technologies to put out the fires. Steve McCurry, a photographer said "There were fires shooting out the ground for as far as I could see, the smoke cloud blocked the midmorning sun." Notice the dates of all these events: they all fall in a sequence: 1914, 1945, 1986, 1990-1991, I believe John is giving us a little more detail in accounts leading up to the Tribulation. Revelation 8:13 "and I beheld, and heard an angel flying through the midst of heaven, saying with a loud voice Woe, woe, woe, to the inhabitants of the earth by reason of the other voices of the trumpet of the three angels, which are set to sound! God says "WOE is SEVEN (7) TIMES IN The Book of REVELATION" 1) Rev. 8:13, He says it 3 Times; 9:12, 11:14

it is said twice, 12:12. (After the fifth angel sounded that was the first Woe; after the sixth angel sounded that was the second woe; after the seventh angel sounded that was the third woe; when God says "WOE" He has reached His boiling point).

Revelation 9:1 "And the FIFTH ANGEL SOUNDED, and I saw a star (angel) fall from heaven unto the earth: and to him (angel/star) was given the key of the bottomless pit. 2. And he (angel) opened the bottomless pit, and there arose a smoke out of the pit, as the smoke of a great furnace, and the sun and the air were darkened by reason of the smoke of the pit. 3. And there came out of the smoke locusts upon the earth: and unto them was given power, as the scorpions of the earth have power. 4. And it was commanded them that they should not hurt the grass of the earth, neither any green thing, neither any tree, but only those men (bad men) which have not the seal of God in their foreheads." (I believe John is getting a detailed description of the Tribulation right after the rapture) (Notice the 144,000 Jews are told not to be touched during the tribulation.) 5. "And to them (sinful people) it was given that they should not kill them, they (sinful people) should be tormented five months: and their torment was as the torment of a scorpion, when he striketh a man. (Job 34:26) 6. And in those days shall man seek death, and shall not find it; and shall desire to die, and death shall flee (run) from them (sinful people)." (Man will try to commit suicide but will not die) (John tries to describe these things that are tormenting man for five months) - John sounds like he's trying to describe an Apache helicopter 1) there wings was as the sound of chariots of many horses running to battle? Hundreds of Propellers humming. 2) Faces of men? Men in the cockpit. 3) Breast plates of iron? Made of iron. 4) Tail of a scorpion? Tail rotor. 5) Teeth of a Lion? Painted on helicopter. 6) Crown of gold? Gold emblem. John was looking into the future and tried to describe what he saw 2000 years away. Revelation 9:10 ...." And their power was to hurt men (sinful people) for five months." 11. "And they had a king over them, which is the angel of the bottomless pit, as many in the Hebrew tongue is "Abaddon", but in the Greek tongue his name "Apollyon"," (often used as another name for Satan.) (Satan or Satan's angel). Here again I believe John is giving a more detail description during the beginning of the Tribulation period. The First Woe Past: Revelation 9:13 "and The SIXTH ANGEL SOUNDED, and I heard a voice from the four horns of the golden altar which is before God, saying to the six angels which had the trumpet, loose the four angels which are bound in the Great Euphrates."

The Euphrates River is in Iraq, northwest of Baghdad. According to the Bible, the Nephilim originally appeared as a result of the sons of God mating with women. Genesis 6:4 there were giants (Nephilim) in the earth in those days; and also after that, when (because) the sons of God came in unto the daughters of men, and they bare children to them, the same became mighty men which were of old, men of renown. 2 Peter 2:4,5 "For if God spared not the Angels that sinned, but cast them down to Hell (Tartarus), and delivered them unto chains of darkness, to be reserved unto judgment; and spared not the old world, but saved Noah the eighth person, a preacher of righteousness, bringing in the flood up on the world of the ungodly;" Rev. 9:14-15 "saying to the sixth Angel which had the trumpet, loose the four angels which are bound in the great river Euphrates. 15. and the four angels were loosed, which were prepared for an hour, and a day, and a month, and a year, for to slay the third part (1/3) of men."(At this time God will kill a 1/3 part of mankind on earth). Revelation 11:1-3 "and there was given me a reed like into a rod: (measuring stick) and the Angel stood, saying, rise, and measure the temple of God (third Temple), and the altar and them that worship therein. 2. But the court which is without the Temple leave out (Muslim Temple Dome of the rock), and measure it not; for it is given unto the Gentiles: and the holy city shall be treaded under foot 40 and two months (3 ½ years). 3. And I will give power unto my two witnesses (Enoch and Elijah), and they shall prophesy a thousand two hundred and threescore days, clothed in sackcloth." Rev. 11:7 when they (Enoch & Elijah) completed the 3 ½ years of their solemn testimony, the tyrant who comes out of the bottomless pit, will declare war against them and conquer and kill them; 8. And there dead body shall lie in the streets of the city, which spiritually is called Sodom and Egypt, where also our Lord was crucified." Rev 11:11 "but after three days and a half days (3 ½ days) the spirit of life from God enters unto them, and they (Enoch and Elijah) shall stand up on their feet; and great fear fell up on them (sinful people) which saw them (Enoch and Elijah)."

The Second Woe Past: Revelation 11:15 "and The SEVENTH ANGEL SOUNDED, and there were great voices in heaven, saying, the kingdoms of this world are become the kingdoms of our Lord, and of His Christ; and He shall reign for ever and ever." - Here John gives the most detail of the Tribulation period in this Seven Trump, even more than the Sixth Trump from the beginning to the end of Armageddon. Revelation chapter 13:1-18 "And I (John) stood up on the sands of the sea, (your Bible should not say (NIV) "The Dragon" for this is Satan. For this was John who stood on the seashore); and I saw a beast (the Antichrist & United Nations) rise up out of the sea (earthly nations), having seven heads (seven hills) and 10 horns (WEU 1. Belgium, 2. France, 3. Germany, 4. Greece, 5. Italy, 6. Luxembourg, 7. Netherlands, 8. Portugal 9. Spain, 10. United Kingdom), and upon his horns 10 crowns (ten kings), and up on his heads (all) the name of blasphemy. 2. And the Beast (United Nations) which I saw was like unto a Leopard (European Union), and his feet were as the feet of a Bear (Russia), and his mouth as the mouth of a Lion (Britain and America). And the Dragon gave him his power, and his seat, and great authority. 3. And I saw one of his heads (one of 10) as it were wounded (Germany) to death; and his deadly wound was healed (Berlin Wall) and all the world (the world watches CNN) wonder after the Beast. 4. And they worshipped the dragon which gave power unto the beast (United Nations), saying, who is like unto the beast? Who is able to make war with him (United Nations 193 Nations)-(1+9+3=13)(13 = Beast/Satan). 5. And there was given unto him (antichrist) a mouth speaking great things and blasphemies; and power was given unto him (antichrist) to continue forty and two months (3 ½ years). 6. And he opened his mouth in blasphemy against God, and blasphemed His Name, and His tabernacle and them to dwell in heaven."

Rev. 13:11 "and I beheld another Beast (false prophet) coming up out of the earth and he had two horns like a lamb (looks like a Christian) and spake like a dragon (sinner). 12. And he (false prophet) exercised all the power of the first beast (antichrist) before him, and causes the earth (all) and them which dwell therein (world) to worship the first beast (antichrist in control of United

Nations/10 kings or Berlin Club includes Germany), whose deadly wound was healed." Rev. 13:16 "and he causeth all, both small and great, rich and poor, free and bond, to receive a mark in their right hand, or in their foreheads: 17. And that no man might buy or sale, save he that had the mark, or the name of the beast, or the number of his name. 18. Here is wisdom. Let him that hath understanding count the number of the beast: for it is the number of a man; for his number is 666."

Carl Sanders, with a team of engineers behind him, with US grant money supplied by our tax dollars, Carl Sanders took on this project and designed a microchip which is powered by a lithium battery, rechargeable through the temperature changes in our skin. Without the knowledge of the Bible these engineers spent 1 ½ million dollars doing research on the best and most convenient place to have a microchip inserted. Guess what? These researchers found that the forehead and the back of the hand is not just the most convenient place but is also the only viable place for rapid, consistent temperature changes in the skin to recharge the lithium battery. The microchip is approximately 7mm in length, .75 mm in diameter, about the size of a grain of rice. It is capable of storing pages upon pages of information about you. All your general history, work history, crime record, health history and financial data can be stored on this chip. Extra! Extra! Read all about it: BBC radio 5 live says "Would you microchip your children?

Two dads who created an app that allows parents to issue any alert if their child is lost, says they are looking into creating microchips for children. They are considering both microchips that could be placed in clothing, and microchips that could be injected under a child's skin that would being an alert when the parents wanted to locate the child. Over 16,000 people have responded on social media after Stephen Fern, who runs the Lost Kidz Company with his brother Darren, sought public opinion on the subject. Despite acknowledging that an implement would be "invasive," Stephen said "over 95%" of people on social media had responded positively to the idea."(John will make a little more sense of Revelation 13:1-18) Revelation chapter 17:1-18 "And there came one of the seven angels which had the seven veils, and talked with me saying unto me, Come hither; I will show you the judgment of the great whore that sits upon many waters: 2. With whom the kings of the earth have committed fornication, and the inhabitants of the earth have been made drunk with the wine of her fornication. 3. So he carried me a way in the spirit unto the wilderness: and I saw a Woman (Rome Vatican City) upon a scarlet color beast, full of names of blasphemy, having seven heads (seven hills) and 10 horns (WEU). 4. And the woman (Rome Vatican City) was arrayed in purple and scarlet color, and decked with gold and precious stones and pearls, having a golden cup in her hand full of abominations and filthiness of her fornication. 5. And upon her forehead was the name written, MYSTERY BABYLON THE GREAT, THE MOTHER OF HARLOTS AND ABOMINATIONS OF THE EARTH. 6. And I saw a woman (Rome Vatican City) drunken with the blood of the saints (Christians), and with the blood of the martyrs (Died for Christ) of Jesus: and when I saw her, I wondered with great admiration. 7. And the angel said unto me, wherefore didst you marvel? (Why are you so surprised?). I will tell you the mystery of the woman, and of the beast that carried her, which had seven heads and ten (10) horns. 8.

The beast that you saw was, and is not: and shall ascend out of the bottomless pit, and go into perdition: and they that dwell on the earth shall wonder, whose names were not written in the book of life from the foundations of the world, when they behold the beast that was, and is not, and yet is. 9. And here is the mind which has wisdom. The seven heads are seven mountains, on which the woman sits. "Seven Hills of Rome" 1. Palatine, 2. Capitoline, Aventine, 4. Caelian, 5. Esquiline, 6. Viminal, 7. Quirinal. / 10. And there are seven kings; five are fallen 1 Egyptians, 2 Assyrians, 3 Babylonians, 4 Medo-Persians, 5 Grecians, and one is 6 Romans (68 AD?), and the other is not yet come 7 United Nations/revive Roman Empire, and when he (United Nations) cometh, he (United Nations) must continue a short space (short time). 11. And the beast that was, and is not, even he is the eighth (8 Antichrist), and is of the seven (7 United Nations), and going into perdition. 12. And the 10 horns which thou sawest are 10 kings (WEU), which have received no kingdom as yet (during the time of John); but receive power as kings one hour (seven years) with the beast (antichrist/United Nations). 13. These have one mind, and shall give their power and strength unto the beast (antichrist/United Nations). 14. These shall make war with the Lamb (Israel), and the Lamb shall overcome them: for He is Lord of lords, and King of kings: and they that are with Him are called, the chosen and faithful. 15. And He said to me, the waters which you see or saw, where the whore (Rome Vatican City) sits, are people, and multitudes, and nations, and tongues (waters). (Rule from Rome Vatican City). 15. And the 10 horns (WEU) which thou see upon the beast (antichrist, United Nations), these shall hate the whore (Rome Vatican City) and shall make her desolate and naked, and shall eat her flesh, and burn her with fire. (Burn "Her" Rome

Vatican City to the ground)."

Pope Francis made a startling admission in Rome on Saturday, admitting that not only is the Vatican a "woman", but that it's also a "mother", he said "and it pleases me to think that the church is not 'il Chiesa' ('the Church', masculine): it is 'La Chiesa' (feminine). The Church is a woman! The Church is a mother! And that's beautiful, eh? We have to think deeply about this."

The Vatican City consumes more wine per capita than any other country. Extra! Extra! Read all about it: Cindy Wooden in Rome writes "Turn to God, Pope asks World Leaders" "the Pope asked ambassadors from the 178 countries that have diplomatic relations with the Holy Vatican. See: Diplomatic Relations Law & Legal Definition: Diplomatic relations refers to the customary diplomatic Intercourse between nations. The Pope travels all over the world having relationships with lots of Kings and world leaders. What do you call a woman that travels all over the country and gets in and out of bed with leaders? A HARLOT or WHORE. The Pope is always in the bed which some world leader and that my friend is a Whore. You ask "Isn't she married to Jesus? No she's committing adultery. "And I heard another voice from heaven, saying, Come out of her, my people, that you be not partakers of her sins, and that ye (you) receive not of her plagues" – Revelation 18:4. Babylon is Fallen!!! "My people, go ye (you) out of the midst of her, and deliver ye every man his soul from the fierce anger of the Lord" – Jeremiah 51:45. Rome Vatican City is referred to as "The Eternal City" or is Jerusalem the Eternal City, which one is the City of God. The Vatican can also be referred to as the Holy City. That title is for one city alone and Jerusalem is God's Holy City.

Joel 3:17 "So shall you know that I am the Lord your God dwelling in Zion, My holy mountain: then shall Jerusalem be holy, and there shall be no stranger passed through (conquer) her anymore." Revelation 17:18 "And the woman which thou sawest is that Great City, which reigneth over Kings of the earth." Rev. 18:1-24 "...after these things I saw another angel come down from heaven, having great power, and the earth was lightened with his glory. 2. And he cried mightily with a strong voice, saying, Babylon the great is fallen (Rome has Fallen), and is become the habitation of devils, and the hold of every foul spirit, and a cage of every unclean and hateful bird. 3. For all nations have drunk of the wine of the wrath of her fornication, and the kings of the earth have committed fornication with her, and the merchants (buyers and sellers) of the earth are waxed rich through the abundance of her delicacies (sensuality)." Rev. 18:10 "...standing afar off for the fear of her torment, saying, Alas, alas, the Great City, Babylon that mighty city for in one hour is thy judgment come. 11. And the merchants of the earth shell weep and mourn over her, for no man buy their merchandise anymore: 12. The merchandise of gold, and silver, and precious stones, and of pearls, and fine linen, and purple, and silk, and scarlet, and..... wood, brass, iron, and marble." Rev 18:23 "And the light of a candle shell no more at all in thee; and the voice of the bridegroom (God) and of the bride (the Church) shall be heard no more at all in thee: for the merchants were the great man (leaders) of the earth; for by their sorceries (pagan worship) were all nations deceived." 24. "And in her was found the blood of prophets, and saints, and all that were slain upon the earth." Revelation 19:2-3 "For true and righteous are his judgments: or he had judged the great whore, which did corrupt the earth with her fornication, and hath avenged the blood of his servants at her hand. 3. And again they said, Alleluia: and her smoke rose up forever and ever."

Remember the Spanish Inquisition and how the Jews were persecuted, God is not forgotten. Revelation 15:7-8 "And one of the four beasts gave unto the seven angels seven golden vials for all the wrath of God, who liveth for ever and ever. 8. And the Temple was filled with smoke from the glory of God, and from His power; and no man was able to enter into the Temple, til the seven (7) plagues of the seven (7) angels were fulfilled." Revelation 16:1-21 "And I heard a great voice out of the Temple saying to the seven angels, Go your way and pour out the vials of the wrath of God upon the earth. 2. And the FIRST went, and poured out his vial upon the earth; and there fell a noisome and grievous sore upon the men which had the mark of the beast and upon them which worship the image. 3. And the SECOND ANGEL poured out his vial upon the sea; and it became as blood of a dead man: and every living soul died in the sea. 4. And the THIRD ANGEL poured out his vial upon the rivers and fountains of water (drinking water); and they became blood. 8. And the FOURTH ANGEL poured out his vial upon the sun; in power was given unto him to scorch men with fire. 9. And men were scorch with great heat, and blasphemed the name of God, which had power over these plagues: and they repented not to give Him glory. 10. In the FIFTH ANGEL poured out his vial upon the seat of the beast (creatures of the sea). And his kingdom was full of darkness; and they gnawed their tongues for pain, 11. And blasphemed the God of heaven because of their pains and their sores, and repented not of their deeds. 12. And the SIXTH ANGEL poured out his vial upon the great River Euphrates, and the water in it therefore was dried up, that the way of the kings of the East might be prepared. 13. And I saw three unclean spirits like frogs come out of the mouth of the dragon (Satan), and out of the mouth of the beast (antichrist), and out of the mouth of the false prophet (religious leader/Pope). (Satan always tries to imitate God (3) Father, Son, and Holy Ghost). 14. For they are the spirit of the devils, working miracles, which go forth into the kings of the earth and of the whole world, to gather them to the battle of that great day of God Almighty. 16. And he gathered them together into a place called in Hebrew tongue ARMAGEDDOM. 17. And the SEVENTH ANGEL poured out his vial into the air; and there came a great voice out of the temple of heaven, from the throne, saying, it is done. 18. And there were voices, and thunders, and lightings, and there was a great Earthquake, such as not since men were upon the earth, so mighty an Earthquake, and so great. 19. And the great city "Babylon" was divided into three parts, and the city of the Nations fell: and great Babylon came in remembrance before God, to give to her the cup of the wine of the fierceness of his wrath. 20. and every island fled away, and the mountains were not found. 21. And there fell upon men a great hail out of heaven, every stone about the weight of a talent (100 pounds): and men blasphemed God because of the plague thereof was exceeding great." Revelation 17:1 "and there came of the seven angels which had the seven vial, and talk with me, saying unto me, come hither; I will show you the judgment of the great whore (Prostitute), who sits up on the many waters of the world. 2. The kings of the world have had immoral relations with her, and the people of the earth have been made drunk by the wine of her immorality."

Let's look at what the Prophet Isaiah says in Isaiah 61:1-2

"The Spirit of the Lord God is upon me; because the Lord hath anointed me to preach good tidings to the meek; he hath sent me to bind up the brokenhearted, and to proclaim liberty to the captives, and the opening of the prison to them that are bound; 2. To proclaim the acceptable year of the Lord, and the day of vengeance of our God; to comfort all that mourn". Jesus Christ quoted the same verse in the book of Luke. Luke 4:16-21 "And many came to Nazareth, when He had been brought up: and, as His custom was, He went into the synagogue on the Sabbath day, and stood up for to read. 17. And there was delivered unto Him a book of the prophet Isaiah. And when He had opened the book, He found the place where it was written, 18. The Spirit of the Lord is upon Me, because He has anointed Me to preach the gospel to the poor; He has sent Me to heal the brokenhearted, to preach deliverance to the captives, and recovering the site to the blind, to set at liberty them that are bruised, 19. To preach the acceptable year of the Lord. 20. And He closed the book, and He gave it again to the minister, and He sat down, and the eyes of all of them that were in the synagogue were fastened on Him. 21. And He again to say unto them, this day is the Scripture fulfilled in your ears."

You see, Jesus Christ was quoting Isaiah 6:1-2. He fulfilled: "to proclaim the year of the Lord." But He did not say the second part of that prophecy… "And the day of vengeance of our God; to comfort all who mourn", but now very, very soon, the second part is going to occur "the day of vengeance of our God", a year of recompense. **Are you ready?**

The prayer of King David is an excellent prayer of a contrite heart that would be good for all of us to pray:

Psalm 51 "Have mercy on me, God, in Your goodness, in Your abundant compassion blot out my offense. Wash away all my guilt; from my sin cleanse me. For I know my offense; my sin is always before me. Against You alone have I sinned; I have done such evil in Your sight that You are just in Your sentence, blameless when You condemn. True, I was born guilty, a sinner, even as my mother conceived me. Still, You insist on sincerity of heart; in my inmost being teach me wisdom. Cleanse me with hyssop, that I may be pure; wash me, make me whiter than snow. Let me hear sounds of joy and gladness; Let the bones You have crushed rejoice. Turn away Your face from my sins; blot out all my guilt. A clean heart create for me, God; renew in me a steadfast spirit. Do not drive me from Your presence, nor take from me your Holy Spirit. Restore unto me the joy of Your salvation; sustain in me a willing spirit. I will teach the wicked Your ways, that sinners may return to You. Don't sentence me to death. O my God, You alone can rescue me. Then I will sing of Your forgiveness, for my lips will be unsealed – oh, how I will praise You."

THE PRAYER OF FORGIVENESS & SALVATION

If you have read this book and you would like to received God's Love, Grace, and mercy and want to become a part of God's family, repeat this prayer out loud:

"Heavenly Father, I come to You in prayer asking for the forgiveness of my sins. All my cheating, all my lying, I admit I am a sinner and need Your forgiveness; I confess with my mouth and believe with all my heart that Jesus is Your Son, and that He died on the Cross at Calvary, taking my place, and taking my sin upon Himself. I believe that Jesus rose from the dead so that I may have Eternal life in the Kingdom of Heaven, and I ask You right now to come into my life and be my personal Lord and Savior and send the Holy Spirit into my life, to You Father for loving me.

In Jesus name. Amen

HAROLD BALL

FINAL COMMENTS

My brother in the Lord, Pastor John Kilpatrick says it best, "this is what the Holy Spirit said "I have many ministers and they are speaking on my behalf but he says, "what is missing is the urgency in their voice."

The mega-churches are really Cognizant, not to offend people and they're really careful when you get up and preach to people, because they want everybody to leave feeling good. Preachers have stopped or are refusing to preach on the coming of Jesus Christ.

"Where is the urgency?" I have never seen America in the place where we are right now. If you think all the persecution is going to remain in Iraq against the Christians, you better think again. It's already coming in this country right now. If we don't tell people what they need to hear, God's going to hold us accountable and their blood will be on our hands.

Whenever we preach we have got to preach with urgency in our voice that we've got to be right with God, if anything should happen to us. There are things right now in motion that could change our nation almost overnight. And for me to stand here and say things are all right, I can't do that! Politicians in Washington may can do that, and lead you to believe that everything is going to be okay. But in the house of God, there has to be a Siren that says BLAST, BLAST, BLAST, ATTENTION, ATTENTION, ATTENTION things are changing and they are changing quickly.

We must have preachers in the pulpit that will say, "Watch out, WARNING, WARNING, RED LIGHT, WARNING!" People know something is going on in the Middle East and they know something is going on in Iraq, Iran, and Damascus. They know about Iran, and people that are not even Scripture illiterate are trying to answer these things and they are they are really missing it.

God is now saying to all preachers, "Get Up And Tell Them!" "It's time to talk about what God is doing. People are seeking the Lord. People are seeking Christ. And if they don't find Him in the Church, where are they going to find Him? I have a final question? **Where is the URGENCY?**

MINISTRY CONTACT INFORMATION

Harold Ball
PO Box 11323
Carson, CA 90749

Email Address:
harold7x7@yahoo.com

Website Address:
www.bibleresearchfoundation.com